365 Days

— OF —

CRYSTAL

Magic

© Jessica Weiser

About the Author

Sandra Kynes is an explorer of history, myth, and magic. Although she is a member of the Order of Bards, Ovates and Druids, she travels a solitary Goddess-centered path through the Druidic woods. She likes to develop creative ways to explore the world and integrate them with her spiritual path, which serves as the basis for her books. Sandra has lived in New York City, Europe, England, and now coastal New England, where she lives in a Victorian-era house with her family, cats, and a couple of ghosts. In addition to writing, she is a yoga instructor and Reiki practitioner. Sandra enjoys connecting with nature through gardening, hiking, bird watching, and ocean kayaking. Visit her website at www.kynes.net.

365 Days OF CRYSTAL Magic

Simple Practices with Gemstones & Minerals

SANDRA KYNES

Llewellyn Publications
Woodbury, Minnesota

First Edition
First Printing, 2018

Book design by Donna Burch-Brown
Cover design by Ellen Lawson

Llewellyn Publications is a registered trademark of Llewellyn
    Worldwide Ltd.

Library of Congress Cataloging-in-Publication Data
Names: Kynes, Sandra, author.
    Title: 365 days crystal magic : simple practices with gemstones & minerals /
Sandra Kynes.
    Other titles: Three hundred sixty-five days crystal magic
    Description: First Edition. | Woodbury : Llewellyn Worldwide, Ltd., 2018. |
Includes bibliographical references and index.
    Identifiers: LCCN 2017036594 (print) | LCCN 2017047804 (ebook) | ISBN
9780738755922 (ebook) | ISBN 9780738754178 (alk. paper)
    Subjects: LCSH: Crystals--Miscellanea. | Precious stones--Miscellanea. |
        Minerals--Miscellanea. | Occultism--Miscellanea. | Magic--Miscellanea. |
Astrology--Miscellanea.
    Classification: LCC BF1442.C78 (ebook) | LCC BF1442.C78 K95 2018 (print) |
        DDC 133/.2548—dc23
    LC record available at https://lccn.loc.gov/2017036594

Llewellyn Worldwide Ltd. does not participate in, endorse, or have any authority or responsibility concerning private business transactions between our authors and the public.

All mail addressed to the author is forwarded but the publisher cannot, unless specifically instructed by the author, give out an address or phone number.

Any Internet references contained in this work are current at publication time, but the publisher cannot guarantee that a specific location will continue to be maintained. Please refer to the publisher's website for links to authors' websites and other sources.

Llewellyn Publications
A Division of Llewellyn Worldwide Ltd.
2143 Wooddale Drive
Woodbury, MN 55125-2989
www.llewellyn.com

Printed in the United States of America

CONTENTS

INTRODUCTION

Popular with Pagans and Wiccans, crystals provide a simple and effective way to add power to magic, ritual, and everyday life. The fascination with and use of crystals dates to ancient times when they served as bling and much more. Through the ages, crystals have functioned as symbols of power, wealth, beauty, and prestige and as tokens of love.

While some gemstones attract attention with their rich colors, others seem to play with the light or shine from within. Many cultures considered certain stones to have metaphysical qualities because their mysterious beauty seemed to echo the forces of nature. Although specific attributes of particular gemstones varied among ancient cultures, there was a universal belief in their protective powers.

Following the tradition of Vedic astrologers in India, early astrologers in Europe ascribed gemstones to the constellations of the Western zodiac. According to some sources, the gemstones noted in Exodus 28, 15–30 of the

Bible was the first ones used with the zodiac. These stones were worn by religious leaders and regarded as particularly powerful. However, due to variations in translations of the Bible and the fact that many gemstone names evolved over time, it is nearly impossible to determine the original crystal(s) ascribed to each constellation.

By medieval times, gemstones associated with the zodiac were shifted to the months. The information on these early birthstones that I have included in this book comes from *The Curious Lore of Precious Stones* by George Kunz (1913, 315), gemologist to Tiffany & Company. Like birthstones based on the zodiac, monthly birthstones evolved. First compiled in 1912, the standard American jewelers' list popularized the use of birthstones in mainstream culture (Kunz 1913, 319). The primary intention of standardizing the list was to get rid of conflicts in older lists of birthstones. Another reason was the fact that zodiac gemstones straddled the months and different sources could not agree on when a zodiac sign began and ended. The jewelers' list has changed over time to accommodate fashion trends, which seems to have brought us full circle to conflicting information. However, because one size does not fit all and everyone's energy is unique, I think having a variety of birthstones provides choices for exploring very personal crystal magic.

This book begins with a chapter of background information that includes preparing crystals for use and charging them with energy. It also provides an overview on how to use crystals. Subsequent chapters take us on a fun journey through the wheel of the year with daily suggestions for the magical and personal use of stones. Naturally, this includes gemstones associated with the sabbats, full moons, and the zodiac.

The Celtic Ogham along with tree months and runic half months are also included. I first encountered the runic half months in Nigel Pennick's book *The Pagan Book of Days* (2001). Like the Ogham and tree calendar, the runic half months are associated with the energy and wisdom of their respective symbols. In each of the rune and Ogham entries, I have suggested crystals that support these objectives. Oghams and runes can be painted on crystals or multiple stones can be arranged on your altar in the form of these symbols.

Other days of note come from ancient festivals. The Romans seemed to have had a celebration for every occasion, many of which related to deities. I have selected some of the festivals that may be of interest to modern Pagans and Wiccans. My main sources for these celebrations were *Handbook to Life in Ancient Rome* by Lesley and Roy Adkins (2004), *Traditional Festivals* by Christian Roy (2005), and *On Roman Time* by Michele Salzman (1990). I have included a few Greek festivals; however, it is important to note that exact dates for these are very difficult to pinpoint. According to British author and translator Nigel Wilson (1935–), each ancient Greek state kept its own lunar-based calendar, which was often adjusted to remain in concert with the seasons (Wilson 2006, 138). Because of this, I have assigned these celebrations to approximate dates.

Even though there seems to be an ongoing debate about angels, I have included entries for working with them. While some people believe they are Christian entities that have no place in Wiccan or Pagan practice, others claim otherwise and that angels pre-date Christianity and Judaism. Because of my personal experiences, I believe that angels are a type of spiritual being that bring messages, provide guidance, and protect us when we are in need. No particular faith has cornered the market on angels; they act regardless of a person's religious orientation. For readers who may believe otherwise, I encourage you to change the angelic entries to a spiritual being of your choice.

Where events overlap (such as a sabbat and change of zodiac sign), you can take your pick of which occasion to celebrate or use your imagination and combine them. Where events occur on changeable dates (such as full moons), activities can be swapped with ones that are not specifically related to a particular date.

Because the date of the "blue moon" (the second full moon in one month) is so changeable, I have not included it within the following chapters. However, when it occurs you can use moonstone, black opal, clear quartz, or selenite on your altar or in spells to draw on its special energy.

Not all crystals or gemstones are minerals from the earth. These *non-mineral* or *organic* gemstones include substances such as amber, pearl, and jet. Although it is regarded as a gemstone, I did not include coral because so many coral reefs are endangered and I do not want to encourage people to support this destruction by purchasing it. If you already have coral, please use it to focus your willpower and send healing energy to the reefs and oceans.

A final word about how to use this book in regard to the number of different types of crystals suggested in it. To follow the entries as written would require an enormous crystal collection, which would require a big financial investment. As an alternative, I suggest using your experience and creativity in determining substitutes. If you are not sure about a certain crystal for a particular activity, take a little time to sit with that crystal and let its energy and your intuition guide you. Not only will this help you become more familiar with that stone, but you will also develop your own self-expression in crystal magic.

While crystals boost energy for rituals and spells, they also strengthen our connection with the natural world because they are created by the dynamic forces of the earth. In addition, the nuances of their individual characteristics enrich our daily lives. Spend a little time getting to know your crystals for a rewarding personal experience and more powerful magic.

---------- CHAPTER 1 ----------

PREPARING AND USING CRYSTALS

No matter how a stone comes into your life, it should be cleaned and prepared—even one that comes from your best friend. This is especially important when you purchase crystals. Cleaning a stone will remove unwanted or negative energy that it may have picked up through previous handling by a number of people. Cleaning will enable a clear, pure flow of energy and help you get the most power from the stone. In addition, it will allow the stone to function more richly and fully with your energy and for your purpose. Crystals should be cleaned separately to keep their power focused on their own energy.

Over time, you may feel that a stone has lost its potency, which is an indication that it needs to be re-cleaned and re-charged. (Refer to the following section on charging a stone.) A stone that has been used to remove negativity should be cleaned immediately or set aside and not used until it is cleaned.

While there are many ways to clean a stone, one of the easiest is to use your own energy. To do this, hold the crystal in both hands in front of your heart. Close your eyes and visualize universal energy running through your body from head to toe. Bring your awareness to the energy above your head. It may help to visualize it as soft white, pink, or lavender light. Feel it gently touch the crown of your head, and then move down to activate your third eye chakra, which is located between and slightly above the eyebrows. As this energy descends to the throat and chest, it activates the heart chakra.

From here, visualize the energy moving along your arms to your hands and into the stone. Visualize the light pulsing and glowing around the stone. Now imagine it moving back up your arms, and then down your spine, legs, and into your feet. Become aware of the bottoms of your feet. Visualize the energy moving from your feet into the floor and eventually into the ground, taking away old energy and any negativity with it.

After cleansing a new crystal by this or any other method, take time to sit with it. Cradle it in your hands and welcome it into your life. Be receptive to the energy of the stone and establish a connection with it by visualizing the movement of energy from your heart to the stone. Also, be receptive to energy coming back to you. After cleaning a stone, there is one more step to prepare it for magical use. This is called charging.

CHARGING A CRYSTAL

When we work with magical energy, we shape it with our intentions through visualization, and then we send it out with our own energy and willpower. Charging a crystal is simply focusing our intent and willpower into the stone to enable its energy to work more effectively with ours. If you have cleaned a crystal with your energy as outlined above, it is already becoming attuned to you.

Place a clean crystal on your altar. Rub your palms together, and then put your left palm on your stomach and your right palm over your heart. The left hand is over the solar plexus chakra, which is the seat of courage and power. This will activate the energy of this chakra and move it up to the heart chakra, which is being activated with the right hand. The heart chakra is the seat of love and compassion. It serves to moderate the energy of the solar plexus, which can be overpowering if it is not in balance with the heart. When channeled together, these chakras produce a flow of powerful energy.

With your hands in these positions, visualize the energy of both chakras expanding and merging. When you feel the energy expand, pick up the crystal and hold it between your hands. Bring your attention down to your feet, and then draw earth energy up through your body. By drawing earth energy, you are tapping into a continuous flow that will enhance but not deplete your own energy. This will also keep you grounded.

Hold your hands in front of your heart as you cradle the crystal. Think of your particular purpose for the stone. Visualize your energy moving from your heart center, down your arms, and into the crystal to give it your intention and to pattern it with your willpower. Continue to hold the stone for another moment or two, and then wrap it in a soft cloth and place it on your altar until you are ready to work with it.

For general-purpose stones, simply think of sharing their energy in your home and magic work. Chanting or singing as you clean and charge a stone helps to raise energy and strengthen your bond with it.

MAGICAL PRACTICES

Crystals are especially helpful to boost the energy of a spell. Whether or not you plan to use one in a spell, place a crystal among the items you prepare for your magic work to enhance and amplify energy. You may also want to store a crystal with your ritual tools to empower them.

Crystals are commonly placed around the home to neutralize negativity and foster protection. Placing stones on your desk at work can be an effective and discreet way to engender harmony or to provide a shield against negative people. Crystals can be placed in the garden to enhance growth or to connect with fairies, devas, and other nature spirits. Crystals also make nice offerings for these magical beings. Gemstones can be used to represent deities on your altar or serve as offerings to your favorite goddess or god.

Just as certain herbs aid dreamwork, so too do particular crystals. Place a piece of amethyst, moonstone, or smoky quartz in a sachet and hang it on your bedpost or set it on your bedside table. In addition, garnet and other stones are helpful for remembering dreams.

Many crystals are particularly helpful for healing. They can be held in the hands for meditation, placed on the body for energy work, or worn as jewelry. Also, arrange stones on the altar of a healing circle to aid in sending energy to someone in need.

THE SPECIAL POWER OF CERTAIN STONES

The shape of some crystals makes them perfect for special uses. Crystals that are naturally pointed help to focus and send energy. In fact, a long, thin crystal can be used in place of a wand. It just needs to be large enough to hold comfortably and point with. Smaller crystal points can be affixed to the end of a wand.

Some stones grow in pairs. These twinned crystals are effective in doubling the power of spells. In addition to twins, many types of stones grow in groups or clusters. This occurs when multiple crystals form from a common base. When used magically, clusters of crystals can provide an amazing energy boost. Crystal clusters can be instrumental for almost any use.

Occasionally, a crystal may stop growing and then start again. In translucent crystals, these growth patterns can be seen as faint outlines like ghostly crystals held within. Known as phantom crystals, these stones are a symbol of the soul as well as transformation. Meditate or sit quietly with a phantom crystal to deepen your spirituality. It may also help guide you on your chosen path.

DIVINATION

You don't need a crystal ball for crystal gazing. A phantom or twined stone or a crystal that has inclusions—internal frost or imperfections—work well for crystal gazing. Sit in a darkened room with only one candle lit. Hold the crystal in front of the candle flame, and with a soft gaze look through the stone. While this method of scrying takes patience and practice, it is a rewarding form of divination. Don't expect to see images in the crystal. Its effectiveness is in opening the mind to receive information.

In ancient times, a simple yes/no divination was performed with two stones of equal size and shape. A brightly colored stone represented the affirmative answer and a dark one the negative. Both were placed in a pouch and after posing a question, one stone was drawn. The process was repeated two more times for confirmation. For your own practice, decide which stone means yes and which means no. Keep them in a pouch from which they can be drawn without seeing them. After meditating on a question, draw a stone from the pouch. Put it back and repeat the process two more times for confirmation.

BIRTHSTONES, STARS, PLANETS, AND CONSTELLATIONS

Wearing birthstone jewelry is a simple way to connect with the constellations of the zodiac. However, there are so many more stars in the sky and we can tap into their energy, too. Since ancient times, gemstones have been used as talismans and amulets empowered by drawing down the energy of stars. We can also tap into the power of meteor showers.

Decide which star, planet, or constellation you want to work with and follow the same procedure as charging a crystal. After drawing up earth energy and bringing the crystal in front of your heart center, visualize drawing down the energy of the star, planet, constellation, or meteors. Feel the energy move through the crown chakra on top of your head. Pull the energy down through your body. Visualize the energy expanding. When you feel that you cannot hold the energy any longer, release it down your arms into the crystal. Hold the stone for another moment or two, and then wrap it in a cloth. Place the crystal on your altar until you are ready to work with it.

In addition to working with star or planetary magic, crystals charged in this way add energy to enhance astrology work. You may also want to consider charging birthstone jewelry for loved ones in this way. Also, charge and attach a special crystal to a pet's collar.

STONES, HERBS, AND OILS

The synergy between herbs and crystals can boost and enhance magical energy. For example, for a love spell combine the use of pink calcite with dill, marjoram, and/or roses. For a spell of luck, use malachite with rosemary, peppermint, and violets.

Oils are often used to consecrate crystals, too. The synergy will boost the vibrational energy of both the stone and the oil. A tiny dab of oil is all that is needed. Avoid bathing the stone in oil as this may subdue its luster and features such as any optical phenomenon.

Now, let's see how we can use crystals throughout the year to support our magic and enhance our daily lives.

CHAPTER 2

January

After the lively revels of Yule, January tends to be a quieter month. This gives us time to ponder the year ahead and view it as a clean slate upon which we can write our magic. This is a good time to take stock of your crystals and plan for new ones that you may want to add to your collection.

January Birthstones

American: garnet (although the rhodolite variety of garnet is sometimes specified, almandine garnet may have been the one used in the Middle Ages)

British: garnet

Others: hyacinth (an old name for a yellowish-red variety of zircon), rose quartz, rubellite (a red variety of tourmaline)

European fifteenth to twentieth century: garnet

This Month's Full Moon

The full moon of January is known as the Cold Moon, Ice Moon, Winter Moon, and Wolf Moon. As the first full moon of the year, it marks a time of beginnings as well as healing. Its power can be employed to attract prosperity, build strength, and foster protection. It marks a time to work with our inner power to develop a sense of who we are and to find our place in the web of existence. Crystals associated with this esbat include moonstone, rhodolite garnet, rose quartz, ruby, and red tourmaline.

JANUARY 1
NEW YEAR'S DAY

Filled with hope for the future, this is a day of fresh starts. An entire year stretches before us like a clean slate upon which we can write our ideas and lay out our plans. What better stone to launch a new year of magic than citrine. Symbolizing the sun, this crystal fosters optimism and abundance. Wake up as early as you can on this day to welcome the New Year. Use this powerful stone in a spell to help manifest your hopes for the year and provide support for any resolution you feel compelled to make.

JANUARY 2
AMPLIFY MOON MAGIC

Associated with moon goddesses, selenite amplifies the energy of the current moon phase and enhances moon magic performed any time during the month. Even if tonight is a new moon, place a selenite crystal on a windowsill that usually receives moonlight. This crystal draws on the cyclic power of renewal, providing supportive energy for new beginnings. Selenite is especially effective for dreamwork and decision-making.

• • •

Because the soft sheen of this crystal
is reminiscent of moonlight,
the Greeks named it selenites, *which means "moon stone"*
(Chang, Howie, and Zussman 1998, 40).

Onyx is instrumental in dealing with the negative energy of other people. Carry a piece of onyx in your pocket or wear it as jewelry when you know you are going to be around a difficult person or someone whose attitude and energy has an effect on you. If the situation with a particular person disturbs your sleep, place a piece of onyx under your bed or on your night table to subdue bad dreams.

JANUARY 4
REQUEST A DO OVER

Unfortunately, there are times when we inadvertently do or say things that hurt someone's feelings. To begin to make amends, light a white candle on your altar and place pieces of chrysoberyl or blue topaz around the base of it. As you do this, visualize what you would like to do and say when you see the person again. Also send loving, compassionate energy in their direction. When you blow out the candle, imagine your thoughts and feelings traveling to that person.

JANUARY 5
AVIAN DAY,
NATIONAL BIRD DAY

Symbolically linked in one way or another with most religions, the bird is the most ancient and longest-associated creature of the Great Goddess. Honor this connection with the Goddess and the wisdom of birds by placing a piece of hawk's-eye on your altar. Also, place one of these crystals on a bird feeder or birdbath to absorb avian energy, and then use it to gain clarity in psychic work or to boost animal magic.

—————— • • • ——————

Many creatures served as symbols of the Great Goddess,
but one of the earliest and most pervasive was the bird.
For a span of almost twenty-five thousand years,
the Divine was portrayed as a woman/bird fusion,
the Bird Goddess.

JANUARY 6
TWELFTH NIGHT

Twelfth Night was originally a Pagan festival until the fourth century CE, when, like many Pagan celebrations, it was adopted into the Christian calendar. Traditionally, this day marked the end of winter solstice revels. Also known as *Epiphany* and usually associated with Christianity, the word actually has Pagan origins. Drawn from the Greek word *epiphaneia* meaning "appearance" or "manifestation," in the Greco-Roman world it signified a deity visiting devotees in a sacred place, often to aid humans (Martimort, Dalmais, and Jounel 1986, 80).

DISCOVER NEW SKILLS

Spending more time indoors during the winter helps us focus our energy inward to study and learn. This gives us the opportunity to develop our skills and talents or discover new ones. Sit quietly while you hold a piece of tiger's-eye, bloodstone, or kyanite. Tiger's-eye empowers psychic abilities and can reveal unexpected talents, bloodstone boosts confidence, especially when developing new skills, and kyanite supports the ability to focus, which helps to enhance and expand our creative skills.

CALL ON JUSTITIA

Dedicate this day to Justitia, a Roman goddess of justice. Write her name on a piece of paper and place it with amethyst, lapis lazuli, or sapphire on your altar to honor her. Also, use these crystals for spells to call on her power when seeking fairness and justice. Amethyst and lapis lazuli make especially good amulets for protection when seeking justice. Sapphire boosts the energy of defensive magic. In addition to maintaining stability and strength, amethyst also aids in achieving goals.

• • •

On Roman coins, Justitia was depicted blindfolded and holding scales and a sword.
This image is still used today to symbolize that the system of justice is fair and balanced in decisions and punishment.

If something is holding you back from doing what you enjoy, make note of it—even just a few keywords—on a piece of paper. Fold the paper as small as possible and wrap it with a piece of yarn or string, and then attach it to a piece of moonstone. Hold this bundle as you visualize the obstacle fading away, and then place it on your altar overnight. In the morning, remove the stone and safely burn the paper and string. Moonstone helps to release anything that is no longer needed.

JANUARY 10
THE POWER OF RED

Even for those of us who love winter and snow, too many gray, overcast days are enough to get anyone down. Shake up your energy by placing red tourmaline or red zircon on the windowsill in a room where you spend the most time. Wearing either of these stones will also help to get your energy moving. Red tourmaline is a stone of action that helps to manifest desires. Red zircon activates energy in the home and is helpful to stimulate ideas.

• • •

The color red is associated with
the elements air and fire and the direction south.
It is linked with the zodiac signs of Aries, Capricorn,
Gemini, Leo, Pisces, Sagittarius, Scorpio, and Taurus.

JANUARY 11
DEEPEN AWARENESS

The darkness of winter is conducive to deepening and expanding awareness. Sit quietly in front of your altar for a few minutes, and then lie down on the floor. Place a piece of azurite or orange calcite on your third eye chakra—above and between your eyebrows. Don't dwell on any thoughts that may occur; simply acknowledge them and let them go. Keep your mind present to each moment and let the stone's energy open your senses to a wider world.

— • • • —

In addition to opening awareness,
orange calcite energizes creativity and boosts confidence.
Not surprisingly, it is associated with the element fire.
This stone's astrological influence comes from the sun.

COMPITALIA, FEAST OF THE LARES

The *Lares Compitales* were Roman deities who watched over particular areas of farmland or city neighborhoods. Located at crossroads (*compita*), shrines dedicated to these deities were the focus of celebrations to honor them (Bonnefoy 1992, 132). To honor your local spirits, create a cross on your altar with pieces of aventurine to represent a crossroads. Aventurine will also help you call on the power of the Lares Compitales for prosperity and well-being.

• • •

Each Roman household had its own Lar,
which was usually regarded as an ancestor spirit.
The household Lar was acknowledged at meals
and whenever a family member entered or departed the home.

THE RUNIC HALF MONTH OF PERTH BEGINS

Perth is a period of illumination when information that was previously obscured from us can potentially come to light. In addition, the energy of this rune is an aid for making choices and solving problems. Draw Perth in the middle of a small piece of paper. Place the paper on your altar with a piece of agate, aventurine, or sodalite on top of it, and then spend time in meditation, letting the energy of this rune guide you.

Figure 1: The rune Perth

If getting your way for a good cause that benefits others needs a little nudge, use hematite to move energy where you want it to go. Write down your desired outcome at the top of a piece of paper, and then list each step needed to get there. Place the paper on your altar with the outcome farthest from you. Position a piece of hematite at the bottom of the page near you. As you visualize each step to your goal, reposition the stone along the list until you reach the top and the desired outcome. Safely burn the paper and leave the hematite on your altar for three days.

JANUARY 15
DREAM A LITTLE DREAM

Place a Herkimer diamond crystal or a piece of chalcedony under your pillow or on your bedside table to enhance dreamwork. Either of these stones will clear your mind in preparation for deep sleep. If you want to stimulate a prophetic dream for a particular reason, hold the stone for a few minutes before going to sleep as you think of your purpose. Herkimer diamond is an aid for receiving messages and for getting in touch with one's inner self. Chalcedony helps to remember and interpret dreams.

• • •

The astrological influence
of both crystals comes from the moon.
While bluish-gray chalcedony echoes the
color of the lunar surface,
the clarity of Herkimer diamond is
like the brightness of a moonbeam.

JANUARY 16
A DAY OF PEACE

Around this time of year in ancient Rome, the temple of Concordia was annually dedicated to peace and harmony. Place pieces of blue lace agate or blue topaz around your home to foster and encourage a peaceful flow of energy throughout the house. This will also have an effect on anyone who enters your home. Popular for its calming and grounding energy, blue lace agate fosters hope, peace, and trust and engenders true friendship. Blue topaz fosters peace and harmony in the home, opening the channels of communication for better understanding among family members.

JANUARY 17
ATTRACT LUCK

This is one of the days that the Romans associated with their goddess of good luck, Felicitas. To honor her, place a piece of cat's-eye, obsidian, or jet on your altar or any special place where you will see it throughout the day. Afterward, use the stone in spells to draw luck into your life. While cat's-eye is famous for attracting luck and wealth, obsidian is instrumental for attracting luck and fostering peace. Jet is effective as a good luck charm, especially in legal matters and for winning favors.

• • •

Closely allied with the goddess Fortuna,
Felicitas was associated with bringing happiness.
In hope of her bestowing good luck,
Roman soldiers inscribed her name on their sword scabbards.
Felicitas was included on the coins of most Roman Emperors.

JANUARY 18
UPHOLD YOUR RESOLUTIONS

It seems to happen every year. Sooner or later, the fresh-
ness of the New Year gives way to regular routines, making
it a challenge to maintain our well-intentioned resolutions
related to breaking bad habits or improving health. If this
happens, take a moment or two each day to hold a piece of
beryl or sugilite and think of your reasons for making your
resolutions. The energy of these stones can help rekindle
and fire up your willpower.

LIFT YOUR MOOD

Long, dark winter days indoors can take a toll on how we feel. Wear a piece of turquoise jewelry to lift your mood. Also, make several little potpourri bowls with dried chamomile, peppermint, and marjoram and include a piece of turquoise in each. Place the bowls in several locations around your home to aid other family members as well as pets. This stone also fosters happiness and wards off all forms of negativity.

• • •

Found and valued worldwide,
turquoise is one of the oldest-known talismanic gemstones.
It was popular with the Mesopotamians, Greeks, and Egyptians.
The Chinese perfected its use for carvings and inlay work.
In Tibet and Nepal, turquoise was used for a range
of sacred and secular objects.

THE ZODIAC CHANGES TO AQUARIUS

This sun sign initiates a period of inspiration, making it a good time to shake things up. Take this opportunity to meet troubles head-on for resolution and change. It is also a time to break free and follow your creativity. Set new goals but don't forget about cooperation and the power of spiritual community. Spells focusing on healing and friendship get a boost from Aquarius. The following stones are particularly effective when working with this sun sign: amber, amethyst, aventurine, hematite, jade, onyx, opal, pearl, clear quartz, sapphire, and red zircon. Red agate, moss agate, angelite, aquamarine, and fluorite are also associated with Aquarius. In the past, jasper was considered especially lucky for people born under this sign.

Associated with the awakening energy of early spring, the power of this Ogham is its ability to activate energy. Luis brings blessings and strength. Draw this symbol on a piece of paper that is just large enough to wrap around a piece of topaz, clear quartz, kyanite, or tourmaline. Tie the paper in place with ribbon or string, and then use this bundle in meditation to foster insight or to activate spells during this time.

Figure 2: The Ogham Luis

SPIRITUAL GUIDANCE

When you feel the need for spiritual instruction or direction, reach out to your spirit guides. Light a white candle and hold a piece of azurite as you sit quietly in front of your altar. Ask your spirit guides what you need to do or know at this time. If you are not aware of having spirit guides, this procedure will help you initiate contact with them. As a spiritual stone, azurite also provides energy for growth and transformation.

• • •

In ancient times, azurite was widely used
as a pigment for wall paintings, especially in shrines.
Later, it was used in medieval manuscripts.

When you have an important occasion that requires polished communication skills, slip a piece of carnelian into your pocket or wear this stone in a piece of jewelry. Just before your part in the event, gently touch the stone or hold it in your hand for a moment or two. In addition, place a piece of carnelian beside your computer when composing important letters or e-mails. This stone provides a channel for inspiration whether you want to stoke creativity or find wisdom.

SEEK CLARITY

If your divination sessions seem to be getting bogged down, keep a piece of clear calcite, clear quartz, or a diamond with you. Place the stone on top of or alongside your divination tools, and then hold your hands above them for a moment or two before beginning your session. These stones provide receptive energy and bring clarity to thoughts. In addition, calcite is the perfect tool for introspection and guidance, diamond aids psychic work, and clear quartz is instrumental for any type of purification.

• • •

Clear stones act as "eye glasses" for the psyche,
helping us see more deeply and profoundly.

FORGIVENESS

Whether you are on the giving or receiving end, forgiveness can be difficult and tricky. For a little help, hold a piece of angelite or apache tear in each hand as you visualize the person you want to forgive or from whom you want to receive forgiveness. Don't reenact the event in your mind; focus on resolution. The energy of these stones will help to smooth the way. In addition to forgiveness, angelite is helpful to foster compassion and generosity. Apache tear makes a good token of forgiveness to foster peace.

• • •

Forgiving is a liberating experience.
It removes the barrier of heavy energy
that can block the soul from finding happiness and peace.

JANUARY 26
ENJOY SERENITY

Now that the holidays are over and the year has come into its rhythm, wake up early and go outside today. Hold a piece of jasper or sodalite in each hand as you enjoy the quiet of the morning. Take a deep breath and visualize drawing peace and serenity into your life. As you go through the day, pause a few times to remember this feeling. Jasper is a stone of peace that provides stability and protection against negativity. Sodalite aids in quieting the mind to draw peace and happiness into your life.

GIVE YOUR SPELLS A BANG

In magic work, there may be some spells that are a little more important than others. For these, include a piece of beryl and pyrite to give the energy that you send out an extra boost. To prepare these stones, place them on a white cloth and sprinkle them with a pinch of sea salt. Fold the cloth into a bundle and put it away until you are ready to use it. When everything is ready for your spell, unwrap the stones as you say:

Beryl and pyrite, my spell ignite.
Send extra power to me this night.

These crystals help focus intention and fine-tune willpower. With a name that means "firestone," pyrite was once used in flintlock rifles to ignite gunpowder (Sorrell 2001, 6). Its energy can give spells a big magical bang. As an aid to concentration, beryl brings clarity of purpose.

THE RUNIC HALF MONTH OF ALGIZ BEGINS

This rune ushers in a time that is conducive to contacting your spirit guides, especially for protection. Hold a piece of amethyst in one hand and clear quartz in the other to open the channels of communication with them. These stones also provide guidance through any issue that may arise during this time. In addition, garnet and onyx are particularly powerful to raise defensive energy through spellwork. Wear or carry any of these four stones as protective amulets.

Figure 3: The rune Algiz

JANUARY 29
TURN UP THE HEAT

Now that winter is in full swing, turn up the heat—but not with the thermostat. Use a little magic. Associated with the element fire, draw on the power of fire agate on cold winter nights by placing pieces of this gemstone around your home. Visualize these crystals blocking any chilly window drafts and creating a cozy atmosphere. Also, place this stone in your bedroom to heat up your sex life. Fire agate is an aid for dealing with problems related to sexuality.

• • •

Fire agate has rich, rusty colors and an iridescence
that gives off flashes of orange.
Its astrological influence comes from Mercury
and the zodiac constellation of Aries.

JANUARY 30
WORK WITH WINTER

Although the days are growing longer, the landscape remains bare and storms may be fierce. Don't feel subdued by it—work with it. Wearing or keeping snowflake obsidian in your pocket or purse can help you go with the flow. Let its energy help you enjoy the stark, wild beauty of winter. Snowflake obsidian is especially effective for protection against people or situations that drain your energy. Also, use it to focus energy for magic and to remove anything unwanted from your life.

JANUARY 31
THE FEAST OF HECATE

Around this time of year, a night was set aside to honor Hecate, the Greek goddess of magic, witchcraft, and crossroads. Acknowledge her power by placing a piece of moonstone, clear quartz, sapphire, or a couple of pearls on your altar. Light a white candle, and then say:

> *Hecate, mother of the dark,*
> *with this stone ignite a spark.*
> *I honor your power and memory,*
> *hail, Hecate. Blessed be.*

In the past, moonstone had the mineral name of *hecatolite* in reference to Hecate (Manutchehr-Danai 2000, 226).

NOTES

CHAPTER 3
FEBRUARY

Named for the ancient Roman ritual of purification called *februum*, this month is a good time to clean and recharge your crystals (Payack 2008, 175). As the night of the year draws to a close in February, crystals provide supportive energy as we await the arrival of spring.

February Birthstones

American: amethyst

British: amethyst

Others: moonstone, onyx

European fifteenth to twentieth century: amethyst, hyacinth
(an old name for a yellowish-red variety of zircon), pearl

This Month's Full Moon

The full moon of February is known as the Chaste Moon, Storm Moon, Snow Moon, Quickening Moon, and Wild Moon. As life secretly stirs underground, this moon helps us find our way and prepare for renewal. This is an opportune time for banishing spells and astral travel. This moon is also a time of purification and working on self-empowerment. Crystals that are especially effective with this esbat include amethyst, obsidian, onyx, topaz, and red zircon. Moonstone and pearls are also associated with this moon.

FEBRUARY 1
THE FESTIVAL OF JUNO SOSPITA

Like a number of deities, the Roman goddess Juno had many aspects and titles or designations. As *Juno Sospita*, "Juno Savior," she was regarded as the protector of the city of Rome (Adkins and Adkins 2004, 263). Call on her powers by placing emerald, lodestone, and/or staurolite on windowsills or tables in any area of your home where you feel the need for protection. The energy of these crystals also fosters a sense of security.

• • •

Juno's other epithets included:
Juno Lucina, goddess of childbirth;
Juno Caprotina, goddess of fertility;
and Juno Sororia, goddess of the protection of girls.

Bringing us halfway between winter solstice and spring equinox, Imbolc is a celebration of the reawakening earth and the initiation of growth. As the world begins to revive from winter's slumber, it is time to shed the past and move forward with hope. Wear jewelry with calcite, jade, serpentine, or zoisite or place these stones on your altar during your sabbat ritual to represent the energy of Imbolc. Also, place azurite or peridot on your Imbolc altar or wear these stones to honor Brigid.

FEBRUARY 3
QUICKEN THE ENERGY OF YOUR HOME

Even though the ground may still be covered with snow, there is a sense of change in the natural world. Tap into this awakening with iolite and/or rhodochrosite to activate the energy of your home. Put several of these stones outside in the afternoon sun for a few hours, and then place them throughout your house to stimulate the flow of energy. Rhodochrosite is a gentle activator that also invites abundance and comfort. While iolite is a real motivator, it is also calming and provides stability.

• • •

Although calcite was the "sunstone" of the Vikings,
they also used thin slices of pale,
transparent iolite as a light filter to help
determine the position of the sun on overcast days.

REDUCE STRESS

If an overloaded work schedule or other demands have you stressed, place pieces of celestine and/or dolomite around the edge of your bathtub before taking a long soak. Use bubble bath or your favorite herbs to make an infusion to enhance your relaxation. Lean back and visualize the stones providing a circle of energy around you as you soak away the stress. The calming energy of celestine brings healing, harmony, and inner peace. Dolomite brings stability, balance, and comfort.

— • • • —

Dolomite is the name of a mineral
as well as a rock containing fifty percent of the mineral.
Along with limestone and calcite,
the Egyptians used dolomite for
constructing the famous pyramids at Giza.

FEBRUARY 5
FOLLOW A WHIM

Sometimes we need to do things on the spur of the moment when a flash of inspiration strikes. If you feel hesitant but cannot sense a good reason why, slip a piece of carnelian or tiger's-eye into your pocket to provide a boost of confidence. Follow your muse and enjoy the depth and beauty of your imagination. Tiger's-eye is instrumental to boost creative inspiration and bring success. Carnelian provides a channel for inspiration whether you want to stoke creativity or find wisdom.

Setting a goal is the easy part—having the will and determination to reach it usually takes a lot of work. Keep a piece of sard on your desk or in your workspace as a reminder to keep climbing because you can reach your goals. When you sit down to work, hold the stone in one hand and rub your thumb across it as you say:

> *Rich-colored sard,*
> *smooth and hard.*
> *Full of wisdom and knowing,*
> *keep my motivation going.*
> *Never to be bored,*
> *I will gain my reward.*

To help your child get over a fear of the dark, place several pieces of jet and calcite around his or her bedroom. Making the placement of these crystals a nightly ritual with your child may help to improve the situation by refocusing his or her attention. As you put the crystals around the room say:

Pieces of jet, black as night,
will keep this room safe tonight.
Pieces of calcite, clear and white,
will shine until the morning light.

The protective and healing energy of these stones will help soothe your child. Additionally, jet is an aid for dispelling nightmares and calcite fosters stability and comfort.

BANISH DOUBT

From time to time, most of us experience feelings of self-doubt. If this happens, hold a piece of chrysoprase in each hand and wrap your arms around yourself for a nice, big hug. Carry or wear these crystals for a day or two as a reminder to not doubt yourself. Chrysoprase is effective in banishing spells to remove anything unwanted from your life, including self-doubt. It is also a stone of the emotions that fosters compassion and balance.

STOP, LOOK, LISTEN, AND FEEL

Life is busy but if we want to develop our magical skills and increase our power, we need to pay attention to the subtle things that are going on around us. Hold a piece of chrysocolla to help you attune to the surrounding energy. This stone helps to raise awareness, hone the senses, and facilitate the reception of wisdom from other realms. With calming energy, chrysocolla is also instrumental in opening the portals for dreamwork and shamanic work.

———— • • • ————

Chrysocolla has been a bit of an enigma because it frequently pseudomorphs, meaning that it chemically replaces another mineral. When this occurs, chrysocolla takes on that mineral's inner structure. This makes it particularly suitable for magic and shamanic work.

If you feel the need for defensive magic, use red jasper to create a protective energy shield. Place pieces of red jasper in a circle on the floor around you as you cast a magic circle. Visualize the energy of these stones rising and creating a protective dome around you. Imagine this dome becoming smaller as you absorb the energy, and then say three times:

Stones of red,
protection spread.
From head to toe,
make it so.

This will also help to repel all forms of negativity.

AN OFFERING TO WATER

This day marks the first appearance of Our Lady of Lourdes, the Lady of Healing Water, in France in 1858 (Lindsey 2000, 93). Honor this gentle, healing aspect of the Goddess by placing pearls (born in water) and opal (which contains water) in a small bowl of water on your altar for the day. Afterward, use the stones as healing charms and the water for your plants. In addition, opal is instrumental for personal insight and when seeking wisdom. Also associated with wisdom, pearls are a symbol of faith and purity that aid in consecrating ritual space.

• • •

Fourteen-year-old Bernadette Soubirous,
who lived near Lourdes, France,
witnessed the appearance of the Lady eighteen times.
The spring flowing from the grotto where her visions
occurred was found to have healing powers.
To this day, it remains a site of pilgrimage.

THE RUNIC HALF MONTH OF SOWELU BEGINS

Representing the energy of the sun, this rune marks a period where we can foster our untapped talents to achieve success and keep moving forward. This is no time for resting on our laurels, especially if we want to reach important goals. To work with and sustain the energy of Sowelu, use amber, aventurine, labradorite, or zircon in charms and rituals. With the help of this rune and these crystals, we can come into wholeness and fulfill our potentials.

Figure 4: The rune Sowelu

FEBRUARY 13
CONSCIOUSNESS RAISING

As you prepare for ritual, place a piece of smoky quartz in your pocket to aid in raising your level of consciousness and awareness for a powerful experience. Wearing it in jewelry is also effective. Because smoky quartz opens a channel for tapping into subconscious wisdom, it provides valuable support for all forms of psychic work. This crystal will also help to keep your energy grounded. In addition, smoky quartz is an effective aid for dreamwork.

• • •

Smokey quartz has been used since ancient times
for jewelry and ornamental objects.
It ranges from smoky gray to brown and black.
The color can vary within a stone.
Crystals with black and gray banding
are affectionately referred to as raccoon-tail quartz.

FEBRUARY 14
VALENTINE'S DAY

This is an important and fun day for expressing love in all its forms. Of course, it's a good day for love spells and charms, too. Especially potent crystals for a little love magic include red agate, amethyst, desert rose, pink diamond, red jasper, and red tourmaline. In addition to whatever else you may do to mark this occasion, create the shape of a heart on your altar with any of these stones to hold the energy of love and romance.

• • •

Herbs to use for love charms with your crystals include basil, cardamom, dill, feverfew, ginger, marjoram, mugwort, nutmeg, saffron, sage, spearmint, and thyme. Flowers include carnation, daisy, heather, lilac, poppy, violet, and, of course, rose.

FEBRUARY 15
LUPERCALIA

This Roman festival celebrated the she-wolf that, according to legend, suckled the infant twins Romulus and Remus, who became the founders of the city of Rome. Make this a day to send nurturing energy to those around you. Wear jewelry with turquoise, jade, or rhodolite garnet or carry one of these stones in your pocket or purse. Visualize your nurturing energy rippling outward as you go through your day. Lupercalia was also the occasion for *februum*, the ritual of purification. To raise purifying energy for your ritual area, use amber, blue calcite, or salt.

Strongly associated with luck and success, green aventurine is a good choice to bolster the energy of a money spell. Wrap the stone with a dollar bill, and then sew it into a small green pouch. As you do this, keep repeating:

May my pockets be full of money
and may life be sweet as honey.

Keep the pouch with your checkbook or financial files. In addition, this stone helps to find and act upon opportunities that can aid your financial bottom line.

CELEBRATE KALI

Although most widely known as a fierce goddess of destruction, Kali is also instrumental in finding truth. Place a piece of tiger's-eye and clear quartz on your altar to aid in working with her. In addition to honoring Kali, tiger's-eye is an aid for calling on her wisdom when seeking the truth in a situation. Clear quartz is influential in summoning her help to make the right decision with the truth you have found. Clear quartz also aids in working with her energy to walk in balance between light and dark.

• • •

Frequently called Kali the Mother,
she is also a goddess of fertility and regarded
as an aspect of the great goddess Devi.
As Maha-Kali, she is the goddess of
time and primordial power.
She has been present since the
beginning of time and will remain
until the end of the universe.

THE CELTIC OGHAM NION, MONTH OF ASH BEGINS

The energy of this period allows us to discover that boundaries are not always limitations because they also provide connections. A fresh perspective on the interwoven aspect of boundaries and connections can help fuel creativity and a sense of renewal. Nion also helps us see that the world is a lot bigger than we may have believed. This Ogham also provides a connection with other realms whether dreaming or journeying. Pale green beryl or aquamarine is effective for working with the energy of Nion. White quartz with iolite can also be used.

Figure 5: The Ogham Nion

FEBRUARY 19/20
THE ZODIAC CHANGES TO PISCES

Associated with water, Pisces brings a period that is conducive for dream and psychic work as well as honing divination skills. It is also a time of sensitivity, compassion, and creativity. Use this period to engage in charity work and magic that helps others. Your endeavors can get a boost from the following gemstones: alexandrite, bloodstone, blue lace agate, fluorite, jade, jasper, staurolite, sugilite, and black tourmaline. Other crystals associated with Pisces include amethyst, aquamarine, cat's-eye, diamond, sapphire, and turquoise. In the past, ruby was considered especially lucky for people born under this sign.

FEBRUARY 20
INTERPRET A DREAM

That otherworldly land of dreamscape is often difficult to remember much less figure out. To help you on both counts, keep several pieces of chalcedony, garnet, or phenacite on your bedside table or hang them from a bedpost in an organza bag. Upon waking, hold the stones between your hands and recall as much as possible about your dream. Writing it down afterward also helps. In addition to remembering dreams, these stones will aid in finding meaning and interpreting messages.

———— • • • ————

Initially regarded as a variety of white tourmaline,
phenacite is also easily mistaken for quartz.
It can have a tinge of blue, brown, pink, or yellow.
Some translucent stones can exhibit a cat's-eye
or four-rayed star when cut into a dome shape.
Phenacite is popular for its intergrown double crystals.

Sometimes we take on too many activities and even though we may find enjoyment in all of them, we can begin to feel bogged down. When this happens, create a circle with rose quartz and/or dolomite on the floor and sit in the middle of it. The energy of these stones will help you to feel free and less burdened. Dolomite is a stone of gentle, calm energy that brings stability, balance, and comfort. The warmth and love of rose quartz helps to release stress.

In ancient Rome, the *Carista*, "Feast of Dear Kindred," was a time to renew family ties. It was also an occasion to make offerings to household spirits. To draw your family's energy together, place pieces of white quartz and dumortierite on your family altar and other locations around your home where your family gathers. Although white quartz provides a link with loved ones who have passed, it is also instrumental for connecting with living family members. Dumortierite opens the channels for easy communication with spirit guides.

— • • • —

In ancient Rome, memories of ancestors were kept alive
in the home by displaying their images in the form of busts.
To Romans, the spirit of a person existed
in the head rather than in the heart.

FEBRUARY 23
A SPELL FOR WISDOM

Write down your reason for seeking wisdom, and then fold the paper in half. Hold it along with a piece of Herkimer diamond, labradorite, or sardonyx between your palms as you send your energy into the paper and stone. Continue to hold them as you think of your reason, and then say:

> *Stone of wisdom, bring insight*
> *for the purpose I seek tonight.*

Place the stone and paper on your altar for three days. Afterward, safely burn the paper and scatter the ashes to the wind.

ACCEPT WHAT
CANNOT BE CHANGED

There are times when no matter what we do—mundanely or magically—we are unable to bring about change. Rather than struggling against the situation, accept it with grace and use your energy elsewhere. Meditate on your situation while holding a piece of apatite, charoite, or quartz. Visualize all the emotions associated with the situation as a big, lightweight beach ball that simply rolls off your shoulders. These stones will aid in acceptance and help you move on with your life.

• • •

Acceptance should not be thought of
as giving in or giving up.
It allows us to stop wasting time
and energy and to put our focus
where it will be most meaningful.

WEATHER THE STORMS

While this often tends to be a stormy month, weather may not be the only thing in turmoil. Sometimes we need help with certain aspects of our lives that feel stormy. Carry or wear agate or morganite beryl to weather personal storms. Agate aids in weather working and weathering the storms of life. It also helps to deal with everyday problems and maintain inner strength. With calming energy that relieves stress, morganite is especially effective for guidance in everyday matters.

• • •

*The color of morganite ranges from soft pink
and lilac pink to an almost rosy salmon pink.
It is dichroic, appearing pink or colorless
when viewed from different angles.*

INVITE HARMONY TO JOIN YOU

For help in bringing harmony into your life, brew a cup of chamomile tea and place several pieces of apatite or moss agate in it as it steeps. When the tea cools, remove the stones and set them aside to dry. Afterward, place them on a windowsill at the front of your home or business to invite harmony inside. Don't throw the tea away. Chamomile is good for plants, so use it to water your houseplants. In addition to harmony, these crystals are associated with abundance.

* * *

Moss agate is usually colorless with green,
brown, or red mosslike inclusions,
which are the source of its name.
Like tree agate, it is sometimes called mocha stone.

THE RUNIC HALF MONTH OF TEIWAZ BEGINS

The rune Teiwaz marks a period that is associated with fairness and justice. The message of Teiwaz is that whatever type of battle we need to fight, it must be done with honor and integrity. Often these battles or challenges are of a spiritual nature. Bloodstone is the most potent crystal to work with the energy of Teiwaz and help you deal with whatever struggles you may face. However, jet along with tiger's-eye can also be effective.

Figure 6: The rune Teiwaz

FEBRUARY 28
WINTER BE GONE

As the number of daylight hours increase, and we long for the warmth of spring, anything that seems to hasten winter's departure makes us feel better. Take three pieces of snowflake obsidian and, if possible, go to a place where snow is lingering. As you toss each stone into the snow or onto bare ground, say:

> Gloom of winter, be gone.
> May spring soon dawn.
> Gloom of winter, be gone.

Snowflake obsidian is also known as flowering obsidian. After tossing the stones on the ground, visualize a flower blooming where each one landed. As each blossom opens, more pop up around it until the entire area is covered with flowers.

FEBRUARY 29
AN EXTRA DAY

Every four years we get an additional day on the calendar. Make the most of it for an extra day of magic. Carry or wear a piece of agate or calcite to foster growth and well-being. These crystals will also keep your energy grounded. In addition, calcite helps to develop and support divination and psychic skills. As an all-purpose stone of protection, agate is especially effective for psychic protection. It also attracts luck.

• • •

An extra day is added every four years to keep the calendar in sync with the solar year, which is the amount of time it takes the earth to travel around the sun. Without adding a leap day, within a century the calendar year and solar year would differ by twenty-five days, throwing seasonal celebrations out of whack.

NOTES

_____

_____

_____

_____

_____

_____

_____

_____

_____

_____

_____

_____

_____

_____

_____

_____

_____

_____

_____

_____

CHAPTER 4

MARCH

Named for Mars, the god of war, March was the first month on the Roman calendar. This is the month when we see signs that the earth is awakening as the bonds of winter are broken. In addition to honoring deities, crystals help us find and keep our energy in balance with the changing seasons.

MARCH BIRTHSTONES

American: aquamarine, bloodstone (traditional), jasper
(traditional)

British: aquamarine, bloodstone (alternate)

Others: blue topaz, tourmaline

European fifteenth to twentieth century: bloodstone, jasper

THIS MONTH'S FULL MOON

This full moon is known as the Chaste Moon, Hare Moon, Seed Moon, and Wind Moon. Its energy helps to coax forth the life that has been stirring in the womb of Mother Earth. In addition to fertility, this period of renewal includes re-dedicating ourselves to our spiritual paths. It is a good time for spells to bring prosperity and success. Crystals that are especially effective with this esbat include aventurine, iolite, jasper, opal, sugilite, and blue topaz. Aquamarine and bloodstone are also associated with this full moon.

HONOR THE EPONYMOUS MARS

With the month named after him, it only seems fair to honor Mars on this day. Second only to Jupiter as a god of war, Mars can be called upon for protection and to bolster courage. Use onyx or sardonyx to help you with these requests to him. The energy of onyx provides protection against black magic and hexes. It also guards against negativity in relationships. Sardonyx is instrumental for cultivating self-discipline and meeting challenges.

• • •

Running for most of the month, the ancient Roman festival
of Mars included feasting and great processions.
In addition to honoring his capacity as a god of war,
it celebrated Mars as a god of agriculture.
Horse-racing festivals were also held
in his honor during this time of year.

MARCH 2
INITIATE RECONCILIATION

No matter how strong a relationship may be, problems may occur from time to time or there may be cyclical periods of unsettled energy. Kunzite or rose quartz can be an aid in reconciling issues and calming the energy between people. These crystals also foster healing energy. Write the name of the person with whom you want to make amends on a piece of paper and wrap it around the stone. Leave these bundled together until the situation or period of unsettled energy is resolved. Afterward, bury the paper in the ground outside.

MARCH 3
THE POWER OF THREE

This third day of the third month is a perfect day for triple magic. It was long believed that three-part things or something repeated three times was magical and carried special energy. Use three crystals to build triple energy. By using white quartz, red garnet, and black agate, we also call on the colors of the ancient Great Mother Goddess. Use these crystals in spells or simply place them on your altar to honor Her power.

⸻ • • • ⸻

Red represents the life-giving blood
of the Goddess and the pulse of life.
White is the color of death, of bare bone.
It signifies the completion of death so rebirth can begin.
Black is the color of transformation.
It represents the soul incubating
in the darkness of the Goddess's womb.

THE FEAST OF RHIANNON

Often honored around this time of year, Rhiannon is the Welsh mother goddess of the moon and the underworld. Although she is well known as a dark mother of death, she is also instrumental in aiding fertility and attracting abundance. In the past, she was a magical figure of the otherworld. Use moonstone on your altar to honor her and to call on her wisdom for guidance. The energy of moonstone also helps to access her wisdom for divination and dreamwork.

• • •

Because of her connection with horses,
Rhiannon is often considered a parallel
to the goddess Epona of the Continental Celts.
Her origins are also linked with Rigatona,
the mother goddess of Celtic Britain.

HONOR ISIS

Around this time of year, the *Isidis Navigium*, a Greco-Roman celebration was held to honor Isis and her power over the tides and the sea. As a way to honor her, place several pieces of aquamarine on your altar as you visualize ocean waves breaking on a beach. In addition, use aquamarine or sea salt for spells and call on Isis to bless you with her wisdom. Closely associated with the sea, aquamarine is a stone of purification that functions well in banishing spells and to initiate renewal.

• • •

From the Latin aqua marina *meaning "water of the sea,"*
aquamarine is reminiscent of the soothing colors
of the Mediterranean. According to Greek legend,
it was favored by mermaids.
The Romans believed it could quell seasickness.

March 6
Hold On to Your Money

When something sounds too good to be true, it often is and we fall victim to deceit. Before spending a lot of money to purchase something or make an investment, sit quietly and hold a piece of pyrite to aid you in making a financial decision. Carefully review the pros and cons and let this stone activate your intuition to help you make the right choice. Pyrite helps to strengthen willpower and manifest intention, especially where money is concerned.

— • • • —

*Also known as fool's gold and monkey gold,
pyrite frequently forms with gold
and is often mistaken for that valuable metal.
Pyrite is sometimes an inclusion in emeralds
and opals, giving them a light golden sparkle.
Lapis lazuli is usually streaked or flecked with pyrite.*

MARCH 7
SUBDUE ANXIETY

Whenever you are feeling overwhelmed, close your eyes as you cradle two pieces of hematite, howlite, or smithsonite between your hands. Breathe slowly and deeply for a couple of minutes, and then hold the stones on your shoulders. Sit for as long as this is comfortable as you visualize anxiety rolling off your shoulders and melting away. The calming energy of these stones will also help you deal with a situation that may be causing anxiety.

INFLUENCE LOVE

Use a piece of dioptase or tanzanite zoisite in love charms to give a romantic situation a little nudge. Sew the stone into a small purple pouch, and then sprinkle it with a drop or two of lavender essential oil. Hold the pouch and bring an image of the person's face into your mind as you send out loving thoughts. Keep in mind that these stones are also associated with truth, so use them wisely and judiciously in matters of the heart.

• • •

With a color that can rival emerald,
dioptase was often misidentified in the past.
Being less expensive, it was referred to
as the emerald of the poor.
Tanzanite ranges from lilac to sapphire blue to violet.
Although rare, it can exhibit a cat's-eye effect.

TAKE TIME FOR INTROSPECTION

Sometimes we need to pause and evaluate how we are dealing with certain situations or people in our lives. To help you, place four pieces of clear calcite on the floor in the cardinal directions, and then sit in the middle. Feel yourself surrounded by the energy of these stones. Enhancing awareness and consciousness, calcite is a spiritual stone that provides insight, clarity, and guidance. In addition, clear calcite aids communication and fosters inspiration.

MARCH 10
SLEEP ON SUCCESS

Dreaming of what you want to achieve can help you manifest it into reality. Before bedtime, light an orange candle and place a piece of turquoise in a small glass of water. Hold the glass between your hands as you visualize achieving success, and then say three times:

Through sleep and dream,
this spell builds steam.
Through water and fire,
I manifest my desire.

Blow out the candle and place the glass with the turquoise on your bedside table.

MARCH 11
CONNECT WITH YOUR CAT

Although our house cats are sometimes just part of the family, they can also be our familiars. Whether or not you do magic work with your feline companion, a piece of cat's-eye or tiger's-eye can help you tune into its energy. When you are enjoying quiet time together, pet your cat as you gently hold one of these crystals against its forehead for a few minutes—if it is willing—then hold the stone against yours.

* * *

*Tiger's-eye is especially appropriate to use
when working with animal and bird energy.
It is formed by an intergrowth of quartz and blue crocidolite.
Unlike its cousin hawk's-eye, tiger's-eye undergoes
a further process of oxidation, which turns the blue to brown.*

STIMULATE CREATIVITY

Place a piece or two of rutilated quartz on your desk or worktable to give your creative energy a boost. When you sit down to work say:

Powerful stone, shine and glow,
stir my energy, make it flow.
Threads of rutile deep within,
may my work now begin.

Say this three times, and then go about your work. In addition to boosting creativity, this stone aids in finding the most appropriate outlet to express your talents.

USE WIND POWER

Known as a windy month, March is a good time to call on the power of air to freshen our lives. Go outside to an open area and take along a piece of ametrine or moldavite. Face toward the east. Hold the stone in the palm of your hand in front of your face and blow on it. As you do this, visualize the wind and the crystal clearing and revitalizing your energy. When you return home, place the stone on your altar overnight.

* * *

*In ancient times, the wind was often personified
as one or multiple wind gods.
In Vedic India, Vayu was the god of breath, life, air, and wind.
The Anemoi were the four Greek wind gods Boreas (north),
Notus (south), Eurus (east), and Zephyrus (west).*

The rune Berkana marks a time of beginnings and fertility. This can relate to a pregnancy and the birth of a child, a new relationship, or the start of a business venture. It can be associated with the early stages of a creative project as well. This half month is also a time of self-renewal and personal growth. Citrine and green tourmaline are especially potent crystals to help you work with the energy of Berkana. If you are planning a pregnancy, use citrine with green agate.

Figure 7: The rune Berkana

THE FEAST OF CYBELE

Worshipped in an earlier time in Asia Minor, Cybele was later regarded as an earth goddess and mother of the gods by the ancient Greeks. Around this time of year, they held a celebration to honor her. To show respect for Cybele, make a circle with pieces of jet around the base of a dark blue or black candle on your altar. Light the candle, chant her name three times, and then sit in meditation. Also, use jet in spells to call on her powers of protection and healing.

• • •

In addition to being associated with fertility and healing,
Cybele was a goddess of caverns, the builder of cities,
and a protector during times of war.

MARCH 16
THE FESTIVAL OF
BACCHUS/DIONYSUS

The purpose of this Roman event was to stir up the energy of nature to encourage the growth and health of grape-vines. Of course, the ultimate purpose was for the vines to produce a bountiful harvest in the autumn. To honor Bac-chus/Dionysus and the power of nature, place pieces of jade, green jasper, malachite, and/or moss agate on your altar in a winding, vinelike pattern. Also, place these stones around your garden or with your houseplants to stimulate energy for growth.

• • •

Although Bacchus (and later Dionysus) was associated with
wine and drunken revelries, he was originally a nature god.
He served as the personification of the sun's power
to make plants grow and ripen.

MARCH 17
SAINT PATRICK'S DAY

While this day celebrates a Catholic saint, there is a great deal of Pagan symbolism on display for us to mark this occasion, too. One symbol is the three-leaf clover. Although it was used by Christians to illustrate their trinity, it was long believed that three-part things amplified energy in a powerful way. Use three green-colored stones such as agate, epidote, hiddenite, jasper, or tourmaline. Cluster them like the leaves of a clover on your altar to give your magic a threefold boost. These crystals can also represent the power of the triple goddess.

Fearn is a time to keep energy grounded for mundane issues and for support while fine-tuning intuition and magical skills. Paint this Ogham on a piece of red garnet or lapis lazuli to use as a charm. To help foster prophetic dreams, place the crystal on your bedside table. Also, hold it between your palms before a divination session to bring clarity. This is also an opportune time to enjoy your uniqueness and focus on the spiritual aspects of life.

Figure 8: The Ogham Fearn

MARCH 19
THE FEAST OF MINERVA

From early Etruscan origins, Minerva was regarded as a powerful force and became a goddess of artisans, schools, and commerce for the Romans. To honor her, place several pieces of blue tourmaline and/or heliodor beryl on your altar. Also use these stones to call on her power for support to develop and enhance your creativity and skills. Blue tourmaline is a stone that stokes creativity and supports the quest for learning. Associated with the mind, heliodor aids learning and study.

• • •

Although a goddess of war, Minerva was also a goddess
of wisdom and keeper of the city of Rome.
A daughter of Jupiter, she was sometimes regarded
as part of a powerful triad of deities with Jupiter and Juno.
The owl was her sacred animal.

MARCH 20/21
OSTARA, THE SPRING EQUINOX

This sabbat is a celebration of both the sun and the earth. It marks the balance of all things: female and male, the spiritual and the physical. It is a celebration of rebirth, as life seems to burst forth everywhere and the earth turns lush and green. Citrine and sunstone crystals are perfect for the Ostara altar to symbolize the sun and its growing warmth. For balance, also place jade or green agate on your altar to represent the earth.

MARCH 21
THE ZODIAC CHANGES TO ARIES

This sun sign ushers in a period of high energy that is instrumental for getting things started. It is a time of vitality, independence, and for blazing new trails. Magic related to financial growth and leadership goals are especially effective at this time. This is also a period for working on assertiveness and developing personal strength. Crystals that are especially effective to work with the energy of Aries include fire agate, bloodstone, lapis lazuli, clear quartz, ruby, and sardonyx. Apache tears, carnelian, hematite, Herkimer diamond, red jasper, and sard are also associated with it. In the past, topaz was considered especially lucky for people born under this sign.

MARCH 22
CLEAR YOUR MIND

With so much going on in our lives, it is helpful to pause now and then to simply clear our minds. An effective way to do this is to sit in front of your altar with a piece of yellow jasper cupped in your hands. Alternatively, lie on the floor and place the stone on your third eye chakra—located above and between your eyebrows. Focusing your attention on the energy of the stone will help clear distracting thoughts and strengthen your willpower.

• • •

Yellow jasper ranges from sandy to mustard yellow or brownish yellow and frequently contains subtle flow patterns or veining.
The Egyptians used it for a range of items, including sculptures of royalty and scarabs.

ENCOURAGE YOUR GARDEN

To give your garden a boost, call on the dynamic energy of crystals to enhance your plants. To stimulate growth, place pieces of moss agate, tree agate, or spider web jasper at the corners of your garden or at the corners of your property. If your garden consists of indoor plants, place one of these stones in each of your flowerpots or scatter a few stones among a grouping of small plants. Also do this to stimulate seeds that you are starting indoors.

MARCH 24
EMOTIONAL SUPPORT

If you feel emotionally vulnerable, wear a piece of obsidian jewelry or carry this stone in your pocket as an amulet to provide protective energy. When you put the jewelry on or the stone in your pocket, visualize a white light spreading and surrounding you as the obsidian creates a shield of energy. Throughout the day, reimagine the stone's energy around you. Obsidian also aids in removing obstacles that impede healthy emotional expression.

• • •

Through the ages, obsidian has been valued
for its hardness and for the razor-sharp edges
that can be created when it is broken or carved a certain way.
Even in smooth, tumbled pieces of obsidian, this potential gives
the stone powerful protective and defensive energy.

MARCH 25
FIND COMMUNITY

When we move to a new house, change schools, or start a new job, it is not unusual to feel shy about fitting in with a new group of people. Carry or wear a piece of lapis lazuli or charoite to help you ease into your new environment. Lapis lazuli is instrumental in building friendships and charoite engenders trust and unity with others. At the end of the day, place the stone on your altar overnight to hold the energy of your intentions.

STIMULATE PSYCHIC ABILITY

Sometimes we can use a little boost to get psychic energy flowing. Before the start of a divination session or other practice, hold a piece of labradorite or danburite to stimulate your mind and activate your psychic abilities. Wear or keep the crystal nearby during your session to sustain the energy level. Both of these stones will enhance your awareness and bring clarity to your readings or other work. Also, use them for aid in further developing your skills.

• • •

Danburite is popular with mineral collectors
because of its prismatic clusters.
Usually colorless, danburite can also be gray,
light brown, pale pink, white, or yellow.
Yellow-colored stones are sometimes marketed
under the name sunshine danburite.

MARCH 27
PATIENCE IS A VIRTUE

From time to time, we all feel as though anger or impatience is getting the better of us. When this happens, take a break as soon as you can from whatever you are doing. Sit quietly while you hold a piece of garnet between your palms. Close your eyes and take slow, deep breaths. As you do this, visualize your feelings as a dark cloud that turns to gray and then white as it finally fades from view. This stone's calming energy also helps to restore emotional balance.

— • • • —

Garnet is a group of minerals that have
related chemical compositions.
Although the name is applied to the entire group,
originally it was used only for red stones.
Garnet was one of the stones Roman naturalist
Pliny referred to as carbuncle.

MARCH 28
HONOR KUAN YIN

In Taiwan, this day is regarded as the birthday of Kuan Yin. While she is celebrated as a gentle goddess of compassion and fecundity, Kuan Yin is also a powerful protector of women. Honor her by wearing turquoise jewelry or by placing this stone on your altar. Turquoise is a spiritual stone that aids in reaching a profoundly deep level. It is instrumental when seeking guidance and wisdom. Also, use turquoise to ask for Kuan Yin's blessing.

• • •

In addition to being a goddess of mercy,
Kuan Yin was also regarded as a bringer of rain
and savior of those who went to sea.
She is also regarded as a great Bodhisattva,
a spiritually advanced person who can pass into Nirvana
but chooses to stay in the world to guide others.

MARCH 29
GET MOVING

From time to time, we all feel as though we are stuck in a rut because the energy of our home feels bogged down. When this happens, carry a piece of serpentine as you walk throughout your home. Begin at the front door and circle through every room as you say:

Serpentine, serpentine,
winding like a snake or vine.
Through each room as we go,
make the energy move and flow.

End at the back door or other exterior door.

Ehwaz brings in a time for focusing attention on progress, especially when it relates to relationships or improvements that we are making in our lives. In addition to these personal aspects, this rune relates to travel. Amazonite and lapis lazuli are especially effective for working with the energy of Ehwaz. Gather together a number of these crystals to create the shape of this rune on your altar. Use malachite or phenacite as talismans when traveling during this time.

Figure 9: The rune Ehwaz

MARCH 31
THE FESTIVAL OF LUNA

The moon goddess Luna was celebrated in ancient Rome around the end of this month. Use moonstone or selenite on your altar or use these crystals to create a special shrine to honor her. Also, use these stones for lunar magic and spells relating to love and romance. The name *selenite* comes from the Greek meaning "moon stone" (Chang, Howie, and Zussman 1998, 40). The word *selene* was derived from *selas* meaning "light" or "bright," just as the Latin *luna* was derived from lux "light" (Anonymous 2013, 90).

———— • • • ————

Moonstone is a variety of the mineral adularia
that exhibits a ghostly bluish sheen,
which is called adularescence.
Capturing the magic of the night sky
with a shimmer that seems to move
as the crystal is rotated, moonstone was regarded
as a sacred stone in ancient India.

NOTES

_____

_____

_____

_____

_____

_____

_____

_____

_____

_____

_____

_____

_____

_____

_____

_____

_____

_____

_____

_____

_____

CHAPTER 5

APRIL

As the weather grows warmer and flowers blossom, it should be no surprise that the name of this month comes from the Latin word *aprilis,* meaning "to open" (Payack 2008, 175). With colors to match any flower and every shade of the rainbow, crystals aid in drawing on this vigorous energy for our magical direction.

April Birthstones

American: diamond, white topaz

British: clear quartz (alternate), diamond

Others: beryl, white sapphire, zircon

European fifteenth to twentieth century: diamond, sapphire

This Month's Full Moon

The full moon of April is known as the Flower Moon, Hare Moon, Meadow Moon, Planter's Moon, and Seed Moon. Under the moonlight, the world becomes a shimmering pool of life-force energy that feeds our bodies and souls. It is a time for planting seeds—physical and spiritual—for future growth and continuity. This moon is also associated with spirituality. Crystals that are particularly effective for this esbat include ametrine, azurite, beryl, kunzite, malachite, sapphire, and zircon.

Also known as All Fools' Day, there seems to be as many versions about its origin as there are pranks played on unsuspecting people. Whether or not this practice dates to Roman times or to the Middle Ages, the tricksters among us enjoy getting up to mischief. To protect yourself from unwanted stunts and hoaxes, carry a piece of onyx in your pocket or purse for defense. This stone also guards against negativity and fosters confidence.

• • •

Herbs that can help boost the defensive power of onyx include angelica, dill, marjoram, mugwort, rosemary, rue, St. John's wort, and yarrow.

APRIL 2
THINK THINGS THROUGH

When you find yourself in a quandary and need to make a decision, write down the pros and cons about your situation. Wrap the paper around a piece of bloodstone, clear quartz, or sphene, and then sit quietly as you hold it between your hands. Take your time and review all your options and their potential outcomes. Do this several times, and then leave the paper and stone on your altar until you reach a conclusion.

• • •

Sphene is one of the few stones with a luster and fire to match diamond; however, because it is too soft to use for rings it is not considered a top-notch gem. Mineral collectors love this stone for its fishtail-shaped twinning of crystals.

APRIL 3
TALK TO THE ANIMALS

For a little help with animal magic, wear or carry a tiger's-eye crystal as an amulet. This will help open psychic channels for easier communication with animals. When you put the jewelry on or place the stone in your pocket say:

Powerful stone, tiger's-eye,
animals run, birds fly.
May their wisdom I perceive,
and with their help, magic weave.

Using tiger's-eye also enhances work with familiars and helps form a stronger bond with pets.

APRIL 4
HOW TO SUCCEED IN BUSINESS

While there is no getting around the work it takes to be a success in business, a little magic can always help. If you own your own business or manage one, use malachite to attract success and prosperity. Place a piece of malachite in a front window or secure small pieces atop the doorframe above the main entrance. Assess the front of the business for other locations that may be appropriate to place crystals. Also, keep a piece of malachite on your desk especially if you handle finances.

APRIL 5
FORTUNA PUBLICA, LUCK OF THE PEOPLE

Around this time of year, the Roman goddess Fortuna was honored at the *Fortuna Publica* festival that was a celebration of good luck. Fortuna was a goddess of luck, fate, and fortune, who had the power to bestow abundance on those she deemed worthy. This goddess could also steer the direction of one's life. Carry a piece of agate or cat's-eye as a charm to attract luck and prosperity. Also, place one of these stones on your altar to honor Fortuna.

— • • • —

As a goddess of fortune and abundance, Fortuna was usually portrayed with a horn or basket of fruit and flowers. Another of her accoutrements was a ship's rudder to symbolize her power to steer people's lives.

APRIL 6
DISCONNECT FROM SOMEONE

For whatever reason, from time to time we may need to let go of someone in our lives. To aid you in this, you will need two small pieces of paper, string, and a piece of sugilite. Write your name on one piece of paper and the other person's name on the second piece. Cut a small hole in each, and then tie the ends of a short string to the papers. Set this on your altar and place a piece of sugilite in the middle of the string as you visualize your connection with the person dissolving.

• • •

Sugilite helps to release attachments and instill a sense
of freedom that invites personal growth.
It is also an aid for transformation.
Associated with the elements water and earth,
sugilite helps to cleanse the emotions while remaining grounded.

APRIL 7
DEDICATION AND DEVOTION

Clear everything from the top of your altar and give it a good cleaning. When you are finished, rededicate your ritual space and altar to your chosen path or deity. Place one piece of charoite or garnet in the center of your altar, and then express your devotion to your deity and/or path. Leave the stone in place for three days before mindfully returning the other things to your altar. Put the crystal back on your altar for another three days.

APRIL 8
FIND PEACE

Taking just a few minutes each day to sit quietly and clear the mind can do wonders for bringing peace into your life. Even if this does not result in absolute tranquility, it will at least help to ratchet down any chaos and tension you may be experiencing. Hold a piece of aquamarine, larimar, or lepidolite as you visualize the clutter in your mind turning into dust bunnies that you simply blow away. Blue lace agate works well for this, too.

— • • • —

Larimar is the blue variety of the mineral pectolite
that is found only in the Dominican Republic.
Its white veining pattern on pale blue echoes the beauty
and enchantment of clear Caribbean waters.
Larimar is also known as dolphin stone.

HONESTY

When issues arise in a relationship, use amber as a charm to build an atmosphere of openness in which you and your partner can communicate with clarity and honesty. Before speaking with your partner, hold the amber between your hands and say:

> *Amber, amber, warm and yellow,*
> *keep the atmosphere calm and mellow.*
> *If we are to remain together,*
> *with your help, any storm we will weather.*

The calming energy of amber aids in healing and fosters stability.

APRIL 10

BREAK A BAD SELF-IMAGE

Unfortunately, we listen to others more often than we should when it comes to self-image. To break through negativity and find a fresh perspective on yourself, hold a piece of rhodonite in one hand and rose quartz in the other. Wrap your arms around yourself and say three times:

I love you.

It may feel awkward at first, but continue this every day until you feel in your heart of hearts that you are a good and worthy person. Both of these stones also foster healing.

CALL ON AN ANGEL

For a special boost to your magic work, call on a little angel power by using celestine or barite crystals in your spells. With a name that means "celestial," it is no surprise that celestine is instrumental for contacting the angelic realm (Oldershaw 2003, 82). Despite the weight of barite crystals, their energy is equally effective for working with angels and spirit guides. Also, place a few pieces of barite or celestine on your altar and around your house or property to raise the spiritual vibration of your home.

• • •

It may be a surprise that celestine
is widely used as an industrial mineral.
In fact, it is an important ingredient in fireworks
and flares because it burns bright red.

BALANCE A RELATIONSHIP

If you have difficulty getting along with a coworker, use a piece of fire opal to foster balance. As its name implies, this stone is associated with the element fire. However, opals are unique in that they contain water molecules, which bring balance to the fire. Hold two of these stones between your hands as you whisper the person's name onto them. Take the stones to work and keep them on or in your desk to help you maintain balance.

• • •

According to folklore, opal was considered unlucky due to a belief that if a stone's appearance changed something bad would happen to its owner. Heating or cracking a stone can evaporate the water molecules inside it and change a transparent opal opaque.

To boost the power of your divination sessions, keep a piece of amethyst with your tools when they are not in use. This stone will clear away any unbalanced energy picked up by your tools during a session. The amethyst will also have them charged and ready the next time you need them. Be sure to clean the amethyst from time to time to keep its energy effective and strong. This crystal is also instrumental for grounding energy before and after ritual or magic work.

The rune Mannaz offers a period of developing goals and achieving success. Through self-work we can increase our knowledge, learn and expand our skills, and employ our creativity to reach our full potential. In addition to advancing ourselves, the message of this rune is that we should foster these same qualities in others. While turquoise is the most effective crystal to use when working with this rune, loadstone, obsidian, and smoky quartz also work well.

Figure 10: The rune Mannaz

THE CELTIC OGHAM SAILLE, MONTH OF WILLOW BEGINS

Associated with the willow tree, the most important lesson of this Ogham is balance and harmony, especially in relationships. The energy of Saille is slow and steady, making room for growth and fostering the ability to go with the flow when necessary. It also helps us learn to listen to the subtle voice of intuition. While ruby is the best crystal to use, calcite and lepidolite together are also effective in working with this Ogham. Hold these stones and meditate on situations where you may need to be adaptable or when you want to tune into your intuition.

Figure 11: The Ogham Saille

APRIL 16
STRENGTHEN WILLPOWER

Rutilated quartz is clear quartz with tiny "needles" of the mineral rutile inside. Before engaging in magic work, hold a piece of rutilated quartz to increase and strengthen your willpower. Stand in front of your altar with the crystal between your palms. Visualize the rutile as your will, strong within you, and the quartz as your energy that will be sent forth. Keep the crystal with you as you go about your magic.

———— • • • ————

Rutilated quartz is named for the inclusions
of golden or red needles of the mineral rutile.
Whenever the mineral hematite is present,
the rutile needles radiate out from the center
in a cross or star pattern.
This type of crystal is called star rutile.

April 17
Fine-Tune Psychic Talents

Whether a talent seems to come to us as a gift or we have to work to develop it, we need to practice and work to become adept and skilled. Like playing the piano or tennis, we only get better at something by continuing to work at it. Crystals are like coaches that help us. Smithsonite is particularly effective for fine-tuning psychic abilities. Have this crystal with you whenever you engage your psychic talents. Also, keep it by your bedside to aid dreamwork.

APRIL 18

PROTECTION FROM NEGATIVITY

When you feel the need to not only dispel negative energy but also protect against it, a handful of apache tears are just the thing to help you. Prepare the crystals by burning a little sage or mugwort in your cauldron. Place the apache tears in a small organza bag and hold them in the smoke of the burning herbs for a moment or two. Because apache tears are usually small, they are easy to tuck away in a purse or a wallet or in your car. You can also leave them in the organza bag to hang in your home.

SPEAK OUT IN PUBLIC

If you feel nervous about speaking up at meetings or giving a public address, let the mineral howlite help you. Make a circlet of howlite beads to wear as a bracelet or to tuck in your pocket when you need to speak in public. Before leaving home for the event, hold the circlet between the thumb and index finger of your dominant hand and gently rotate it, touching each bead. This stone will help to reduce anxiety and stress. Howlite is also a memory aid.

• • •

Howlite is sometimes called white turquoise
because of its similar veining pattern.
Mineral collectors are fond of the cauliflower-like
clumps that howlite sometimes forms.
Mainly used for beads, jewelry, and ornamental objects,
it is often carved into the shape of a skull.

APRIL 20/21
THE ZODIAC CHANGES TO TAURUS

This is a period during which love and money spells are particularly effective because whatever is started now tends to last. Creative work is enhanced because of the vitality and passionate nature of Taurus. This is also a time of sensuality and pleasure that is balanced by grounded stability and determination. Crystals that are especially effective to support the energy of this sun sign include tree agate, chrysocolla, chrysoprase, emerald, iolite, red jasper, kunzite, lapis lazuli, opal, pyrite, sapphire, selenite, turquoise, and zircon. Other stones associated with Taurus include carnelian, diamond, moss agate, and rhodonite. In the past, garnet was considered especially lucky for people born under this sign.

WATER POWER

You may need to swap this rainy-day activity with another entry to use the power of April showers. Fill a clear glass bowl halfway with aquamarine, clear calcite, larimar, and selenite. Sprinkle a pinch of sea salt over the crystals, and then place the bowl outside where it will catch rain. When the bowl is almost full, bring it inside, dry off the outside of it, and place it on your altar. Use the water to power spells and consecrate divination tools. It will be especially powerful when used to represent water in ritual.

• • •

*Other crystals associated with water include
amethyst, angelite, azurite, blue lace agate,
fluorite, jade, labradorite, lapis lazuli, lepidolite,
moonstone, opal, sapphire, sodalite, sugilite, blue topaz,
blue and watermelon tourmaline, and turquoise.*

APRIL 22
EARTH DAY

Begun in 1970, Earth Day is now commemorated around the world. Celebrate the beauty and wonder of our planet by taking part in activities that give back to the earth. After all, she is the mother that nourishes us with her bounty and goodness. Also, mark the occasion with mindfulness and respect by placing brown agate, moss agate, andalusite, bloodstone, citrine, or diopside on your altar or outdoors around your property.

GAIN INSIGHT

For help in figuring out a situation or a feeling that is confounding you, call on a crystal ally. Sit quietly where you will not be disturbed and hold a piece of cat's-eye against your third eye chakra, which is located between and slightly above your eyebrows. At first, you may not fully understand the information you receive, but the insight gained will help point you in the right direction. As a stone of intuition, cat's-eye is also effective for stimulating awareness.

• • •

Although a number of stones such as ruby, tourmaline,
and others can produce a cat's-eye effect,
chrysoberyl exhibits it most strikingly
and is the only one rightfully known
simply as cat's-eye without reference to the type of mineral.
Quartz cat's-eye also produces a strong effect.

NEW FRIENDS

Moving to a new home in a new town is exciting but it comes with some challenges, especially when it involves a long distance that puts you far away from old friends. Fitting in and building community takes effort and time. Wear sard jewelry or carry a piece of this stone in your pocket or purse to aid you in finding community and in making new friends. Sard is also a stone of courage, which can help you get over any initial shyness.

• • •

Used for engraved jewelry since antiquity,
sard is a reddish brown variety of carnelian.
Sard was a favorite of Etruscan gem cutters
who used it for cameos depicting deities,
warriors, and the mythical sphinx.
In the Middle Ages, a piece of sard jewelry was believed
to protect the wearer against sorcery.

APRIL 25
BOOST YOUR SEX LIFE

If you feel the need to revitalize your sex life, prepare a piece of smoky quartz by dabbing a little rose and clove essential oils on it. As you do this say:

Power of quartz, smoky and dark,
with your magic my sex life spark.
Bring love, excitement, and harmony,
this is my will, so mote it be.

Place the stone in a sachet and attach it to the opposite side of your bed's headboard, where it will not be visible.

Respecting other people is important and so is respecting ourselves. If you find that your self-respect needs a boost, hold a piece of chrysoberyl every morning when you wake up and say:

Chrysoberyl, stone of powerful effect,
support my quest to build respect.

This stone also increases respect for others. In addition to fostering a deep-seated sense of confidence, chrysoberyl brings optimism and peace of mind.

Sometimes after reaching a decision, obstacles may seem to appear suddenly to prevent us from staying the course to achieve a goal. If this happens, a little crystal magic can boost your determination. Cradle a piece of red agate in both hands as you stand in front of your altar and say:

> *Agate of red with swirling bands,*
> *I remain determined on this stand.*
> *May your energy create a shield*
> *to help me stay firm and not yield.*

Repeat this anytime you feel that something is getting in the way of reaching your goal.

APRIL 28
FLORALIA

The Roman celebration of *Floralia*, which took place around this time of year, was named for Flora, the goddess of spring and flowers. Celebration at this festival of fertility was usually expressed through sexual practices. This is a good time to call on Flora for spells involving love, lust, and fertility. Use green jasper for fertility, pink jasper for love, and carnelian for lust. All of these crystals can be combined with a few drops of rose essential oil for an extra boost.

• • •

Flora was regarded as the female counterpart
and complement to Faunus, the Roman god of fertility
and nature. Not surprisingly, the Latin term "flora and fauna"
refers to plant and animal life.

THE RUNIC HALF MONTH OF LAGUZ BEGINS

Associated with the element water, the energy of the Laguz half month centers on fertility, creativity, and emotional balance. This is a dynamic time when life seems to flow and magic work can be exceptionally powerful. Moss agate is particularly potent for tapping into the energy of this rune, especially for balancing energy and emotions. Jade is particularly effective for supporting fertility and creative energy. Rose quartz along with green aventurine or smoky quartz are also effective.

Figure 12: The rune Laguz

NATIONAL ARBOR DAY

This day focuses on revitalizing forestland and planting more trees in cities and towns. In addition to taking part in activities to plant or take care of trees, this is a good time to send out magical energy to support the green world. Of course, today is an opportunity to visit your favorite tree or woods. Leave a piece of tree agate or tumbled petrified wood with a special tree to express your appreciation for it.

——— • • • ———

Looking like a design on a frosty window,
tree agate can be colorless, gray, or white
with dark patterns that often resemble a branching tree.
It is also known as dendritic agate and mocha stone.

CHAPTER 6

MAY

With the earth turning into a lush garden of color, it is no surprise that May is called a magical month. In addition, this month is strongly associated with the fairy folk. Aiding in all forms of fertility and growth, crystals are also the perfect gift for fairies and plant devas.

May Birthstones

American: agate, emerald (traditional)

British: chrysoprase (alternate), emerald

Others: carnelian, chalcedony, tourmaline, tsavorite
(a variety of green garnet)

European fifteenth to twentieth century: agate, emerald

This Month's Full Moon

The full moon of May is known as the Flower Moon, Fairy Moon, Milk Moon, and Hare Moon. With life and beauty bursting forth all around us, we can see why this moon is associated with fertility, love, and well-being. This period of enchantment also enhances divination skills. Crystals that are especially effective with this esbat include agate, carnelian, tsavorite garnet, rose quartz, and tourmaline. For help working with the fairies, use amber, diopside, peridot, or staurolite crystals.

This sabbat is a celebration of the union of the Goddess and God, of fertility, new life, and growth. The most widespread and enduring of Beltane rituals is the dance around the Maypole, which symbolically represents male virility and fertility. To enhance the energy of your sabbat ritual, set up a circular crystal grid on your altar with amazonite, garnet, jasper, and/or rose quartz. If you have a long crystal, set it upright in a small bowl of sand to represent the Maypole.

MAY 2
TAKE AN ASTRAL JOURNEY

While the veil between the worlds is still thin after Beltane, this is an opportune time for astral work and journeying. As an aid, place a quartz crystal in a small pouch and attach it to your belt or put it in your pocket. Alternatively, place it by your feet as you journey. This stone is especially powerful for traversing the realms. It will keep your energy grounded and aid in a smooth return to this realm.

• • •

Quartz can be bluish white, brown, colorless, gray blue,
green, pink, purple, rose, violet, white, or yellow.
While intergrown twins are common,
quartz crystals more often form clusters.
Single crystals are sometimes doubly terminated.

MAY 3
CELEBRATE THE GOOD GODDESS

In addition to being a goddess of fertility and growth, Maia was also known as the *Bona Dea*, "Good Goddess," who symbolized "the fecund power of love" (Roy 2005, 281). Around this time of year, the women of Rome celebrated her. Place green agate, green garnet, or zoisite on your altar for a ritual, or place these crystals on a table at an informal gathering of women to energetically connect with the Goddess.

MAY 4
ENHANCE YOUR MEMORY

With so much going on in our lives, we can usually use a little help remembering things. Chalcedony, howlite, and sugilite are effective aids to enhance and strengthen memory. Hold one of these stones while you are reading or place it with your books while studying. If you are using a computer, place the stone on top of the monitor or beside the keyboard. For help at school, carry one of these stones in your pocket while taking an exam.

• • •

Chalcedony was named for Chalcedon,
an ancient port city near present-day Istanbul, Turkey.
Greek sailors used it as an amulet to protect them from drowning.
During the Middle Ages, it was believed to have
the power to ward off ghosts.

MAY 5
WISH UPON A SHOOTING STAR

The Eta Aquarid meteor showers occur when the earth passes through dust released by the famous Halley's Comet. This brilliant nighttime show usually peaks around May 5 or 6. Because of their appearance, meteors have been called shooting or falling stars. The idea of making a wish on a shooting star dates to ancient Greece as noted by astronomer Ptolemy. It was believed that the gods were rearranging the heavens so they could peer down to earth, which made it an opportune time for mortals to send up wishes and requests. Hold a piece of garnet or tourmaline when you go outside to look for meteors and make a wish when you see the first one.

MAY 6 AND 7
HAPPY BIRTHDAY,
APOLLO AND ARTEMIS

Held around this time of year in ancient Greece, the *Thargelia* was a two-day celebration marking the birthdays of brother and sister Apollo and Artemis. To honor these deities with their respective celestial associations, place a circle of sunstone crystals for Apollo and a circle of moonstone for Artemis on your altar. Afterward, use these stones to add solar and lunar power to magic work or ritual.

• • •

The formidable twin deities of Greek mythology, Artemis and Apollo were the product of Zeus's indiscretion with Leto. The island of Delos in the Aegean Sea, the place of their birth, was regarded as one of the most sacred sites in the Greek world.

STICK TO IT

If you need a little help in cultivating self-discipline, sardonyx can provide some support. This stone is an aid for breaking bad habits and developing practices or routines that are beneficial and healthy. When dealing with bad habits, roll the stone between your fingers to help focus your thoughts elsewhere. Also spend a little time holding the stone as you visualize how you want to change things in your life. The energy of sardonyx engenders cheerfulness, which helps maintain a positive attitude.

MAY 9
FACE THE PAST

Crystals can aid past-life work and support coming to terms with things from the past that may arise in your current life. Before a past-life session or meditation, hold a piece of petrified wood, white quartz, or cuprite with both hands in front of your heart. Feel the energy of the stone fill your heart with soft, gentle energy. These crystals will provide supportive energy and help you handle issues that may relate to the past.

• • •

Petrified wood is found worldwide,
especially in areas where volcanoes have erupted.
Wood from the petrified forest near Chemnitz, Germany,
came to be known as star stones because of the starlike pattern
found in cross-sections of tree trunks and branches.

MAY 10
DEAL WITH A LOSS

Unfortunately, things do not always go according to plan and we suffer a loss. Some of these may be big and require reaching out to others and some may be small, but we experience their effects nonetheless. Ametrine or rose quartz can provide soothing and supportive energy to help you cope. Spend a little time each day to sit quietly while you hold one of these stones. These crystals will help you recover and move forward.

MAY 11

DON'T LET ENERGY VAMPIRES BITE

Whether or not we think of certain people as vampires, we all know at least one person whose presence seems to drain our energy. One way to fight back is with snowflake obsidian. Carry or wear this stone when you are around that person. Touch the crystal and visualize its energy forming a shield around you. If the energy vampire is a coworker, keep this stone in your desk at work for protection.

— • • • —

Another way to stop energy vampires is to hold the crystal between your hands as you visualize snow falling on the person and freezing their energy so it cannot reach you.

EMPOWER YOUR EMOTIONS

As much as we may try to maintain an even keel, emotional ups and downs are a regular part of life. During the times when you need support and empowerment, wear a pendant of azurite. Near your heart, this stone will bring stability and validity to your feelings. For extra help, touch the stone with your fingertips to activate its energy or gaze at its soothing color. Azurite also aids in removing obstacles.

• • •

Associated with the element water, azurite is deep blue. However, it is a pleochroic stone, which means it can appear different shades of color when viewed from different angles.

THE CELTIC OGHAM HUATH, MONTH OF HAWTHORN BEGINS

The Ogham Huath ushers in a period of healing and hope. It is also a time for dealing with obstacles and stoking spiritual energy. Huath is a symbol of prosperity, of enchantment, and of approaching summer. To connect with the power of Huath, place lapis lazuli, blue lace agate, or fluorite under a hawthorn tree. Alternatively, sit in front of your altar as you hold one of these stones and visualize a hawthorn tree in bloom.

Figure 13: The Ogham Huath

The energy of the rune Inguz focuses on the family and home, especially protecting the home and property. Although Inguz supports individual growth, it also shows us that the love and warmth of family helps bring success. Also associated with male fertility, Inguz provides a time for men to evaluate their roles as fathers and caregivers. Calcite, garnet, and jasper are especially effective for working with the energy of this rune.

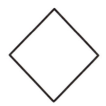

Figure 14: The rune Inguz

MAY 15
HONOR MERCURY

The *Mercuralia*, a celebration to honor the god Mercury, was held around this time of year in ancient Rome. Mercury was the god of merchants, the protector of roads and travelers, and a messenger to other gods. Place several aquamarine or phenacite crystals on your altar to honor him. Also, use these stones as amulets to call on his help for travel protection or to aid in clear communication. Also associated with Mercury, emerald and malachite are effective in spells for business success.

• • •

Ancient writers noted that Mercury was a humorous deity who was also cunning and shrewd. In addition to protecting roads, he presided over the construction of them. In some legends, he played a role in the founding of Rome.

MAY 16
SOMEWHERE OVER THE RAINBOW

You may need to swap this entry with another day. If it rains, go out and look for a rainbow. When you find one, hold a piece of rainbow obsidian and make a wish. Afterward, say three times:

Stone of many colors and hues,
bring the wish that I now choose.

When you return home, place the stone on your altar for three days. Expanding awareness and heightening the senses, rainbow obsidian aids in connecting with the natural world.

HEAL A RIFT

When bad feelings occur with someone and you want to close the gulf that may have developed, use blue apatite, beryl, or kunzite as a peace offering to smooth the way. If the other person is someone with whom you live, place a couple of these stones in various common areas of the house. If you do not live with that person, write his or her name on a piece of paper and place it in a sachet with the stone. Take the sachet with you when you are with that person. These stones will also bring peace and healing to the relationship.

BRING SPIRITUAL BALANCE

Like many aspects of life, we also need to work on spiritual balance. Whenever this part of life seems a little off-kilter, take a piece of apophyllite, desert rose, diopside, or quartz with you to your favorite outdoor place. Spend a few minutes tuning into the natural world while holding the stone between your hands. Visualize its energy moving up your arms to your heart, and then throughout your body. Be aware of the energy finally moving down to your feet to ground and center you.

• • •

Apophyllite crystals can take the form of cubes or rectangular prisms that terminate in four-sided pyramids. Collectors especially like apophyllite for its clusters of upright crystals that form a spray or fan-shaped array.

Don't just wish and dream for better things to come into your life, let the energy of a crystal help you. Malachite is one of the best stones to use in spells to attract money and boost prosperity. Wrap a dollar bill around a piece of malachite and say three times:

Stone of green wrapped in this bill,
hear my call, my wish fulfill.

Continue to hold the stone as you visualize how you would like to manifest prosperity in your life.

Making changes in our lives can be a challenge. Even positive changes can be disruptive and cause some amount of turmoil. When this happens, rhodochrosite is a stone that offers support during times of change. Wear it in a piece of jewelry or keep a small strand of rhodochrosite beads in your pocket or purse. The energy of this stone will provide support and stability during the transition. Rhodochrosite also aids in balancing the emotions.

——— • • • ———

Rhodochrosite received little attention outside the mineralogy world until concentrically banded pieces called Inca rose were introduced to the public. The roselike pattern of Inca rose is revealed when a stalagmite or stalactite of rhodochrosite is cut in cross-section.

This is a period focused on adaptability, changes, communication, and creativity. Stay alert and use the knowledge at hand to work out problems or to get to the truth of a situation. Crystals that are especially effective with this sun sign include tree agate, aquamarine, cat's-eye, chrysocolla, citrine, lodestone, serpentine, and topaz. These stones will also boost the power of your magic work and enhance divination during this time. Other crystals associated with Gemini include howlite, moss agate, clear quartz, tiger's-eye, and watermelon tourmaline. In the past, emerald was considered especially lucky for people born under this sign.

DO NOT DISTURB

As much as we need to be around family and friends, there are other times when we need to be alone. Ironically, it often seems as though this is when everyone wants our attention. To remedy the situation, hold a clear quartz crystal as you visualize it creating a shield of energy around you to function as a gentle "do not disturb" sign. When you are ready to rejoin the world, run cold water over the stone and imagine its energy around you dissipating.

• • •

Also called rock crystal, this variety of quartz has been associated with healing and divination for thousands of years. Clear quartz crystals have been integral to shamanism almost worldwide.

ROSALIA, ROSES TO HONOR

The Rosalia was a family occasion in ancient Rome when roses were placed on the graves of loved ones to honor and remember them. You can use fresh flowers or dab a little bit of rose essential oil on several pieces of rose quartz or a desert rose cluster. Place the stones on your altar along with a picture of deceased family members to symbolically honor them with roses. The Inca rose variety of rhodochrosite can also be used.

• • •

Roses were frequently mentioned in Roman inscriptions as offerings to the dead as a pledge of eternal spring in the afterlife. Roses were painted on the walls of tombs because the color represented blood and ongoing life.

THE CALLYNTERIA OF ATHENA

Held during the spring, this occasion marked the cleaning of Athena's temple on the Acropolis in Athens. The floors were swept, adornments on the statues washed, and the temple purified. Use this day to clean and change up your altar and ritual space. When you are finished, place pieces of celestine or jasper on your clean altar to honor Athena. For spells to call on her wisdom for courage, defense, or justice, use garnet, jade, or brown tourmaline.

This is one of several Roman celebrations to honor and call on the power of the goddess Fortuna. Use it as a day for working spells to bring good luck with green aventurine, chrysoprase, and/or green jasper. Place several of these stones in a small sachet, and then hold it between your hands as you say:

> *Beautiful Fortuna,*
> *shine bright as Luna.*
> *I call on you this day*
> *to bring good things my way.*

Carry the sachet with you for the day and then place it on your altar overnight.

CONNECT WITH YOUR SPIRIT GUIDES

While particular spirit guides may sometimes come and go in our lives, there are always some spirit beings with us at all times. Crystals help us tune into their realm to meet new guides or contact the ones with whom we are familiar. Sit quietly in front of your altar or other special place and hold a piece of dumortierite, jade, labradorite, or phenacite. These crystals will help open energy channels to contact your guides. They will also help you receive and understand communications from your spirit guides.

— • • • —

While we may think of jade as only one type of stone,
there are two types: jadeite and nephrite.
Nephrite is the jade that was used in ancient China for sacred
and secular carvings. It was regarded as the stone of heaven.

MAY 27
ENHANCE THE ENCHANTMENT

I think most people would agree that May is a particularly enchanting month with warming weather and blooming gardens. To enhance your experience of this month, sit outside after dark while you hold a cluster of aragonite crystals in your hands. Enjoy the scents and sounds of this magical month as you visualize the crystals absorbing the energy of the natural world. Later in the year, hold these crystals whenever you want to experience the magic of May.

• • •

Aragonite usually forms long, thin crystals
that are frequently twinned.
Multiple crystals often form structures called sixlings,
which can have a starlike shape.
The aragonite formation called flos-ferri, *"flowers of iron,"*
looks like branching coral (Koehler 2007, 262).

MAY 28
FOSTER INNER PEACE

Sometimes we can all use a little help to foster and maintain inner peace. Celestine, larimar, and rose quartz are especially helpful for this. Wear any of these crystals as a pendant so it will be near your heart. Whenever you feel a little flustered or uncertain, touch the stone for a moment or two to connect with it as you visualize being surrounded by calm, peaceful energy. Earrings that include these crystals help to bring peace of mind.

The energy of the Othila rune is associated with heritage, the home, and ancestral lands. The prosperity associated with this period of time is concerned with the rich spiritual and cultural heritage that provides the foundation of who we are. To honor all of the things—material, physical, spiritual—that you have inherited, place pieces of calcite or malachite with objects that were handed down to you. Contemplate how all of these inheritances have made you uniquely you.

Figure 15: The rune Othila

MAY 30

COMMUNICATE WITH ANGELS

Angelite is the perfect stone for opening the channels of communication with angels. You will need six pieces of angelite to do this. Lay out the stones where you will lie down on the floor or on your bed. Arrange five of the stones in a semicircle where you will place your head. Once you lie down, place the sixth piece on your chest. Focus your mind on the energy of the stones and listen with your heart.

— • • • —

Although alabaster was a favored material for carvings
in ancient Egypt, second on their list was white
or pale blue anhydrite.
This stone earned the common name
of angelite because its shade of blue
is regarded as a heavenly color.

REPEL NEGATIVE ENERGY

While crystals help us deal with negative energy in the home, we can stay ahead of the game by keeping it from entering. To dispel negativity on your front doorstep, sprinkle a handful of sea salt under the welcome mat. As you do this say:

> *From the sea, mineral salt,*
> *bring negativity to a halt.*
> *Let only goodness enter here;*
> *keep this home full of cheer.*

For other exterior doors, repeat the incantation as you sprinkle a pinch of salt across each threshold.

CHAPTER 7

JUNE

The month of June was named for the Roman goddess Juno. Because she was considered a goddess of marriage, June has been a popular month in which to tie the knot or jump the broomstick. Gemstones and crystals, of course, make perfect wedding or anniversary gifts.

JUNE BIRTHSTONES

American: alexandrite, moonstone (traditional), pearl
   (traditional)

British: alexandrite (alternate), moonstone, pearl

Others: chalcedony, emerald, opal

European fifteenth to twentieth century: agate, cat's-eye,
   turquoise

THIS MONTH'S FULL MOON

The full moon of June is known as the Dyad Moon, Honey
Moon, Mead Moon, and Strawberry Moon. This esbat is
a celebration of sweet abundance as we enjoy the gentle
warmth of this season. It is also a time of love and relationships, especially marriage. This esbat is an opportune
time for prosperity spells. Crystals that support the energy
of this moon include agate, cat's-eye, chrysoberyl, emerald,
ruby, and smoky quartz. Alexandrite, garnet, and moonstone are also associated with this esbat.

CELEBRATE JUNO MONETA

Juno Moneta, whose name means "money" in Latin, was the patron deity of the city of Rome (Skeat 1993, 291). Presiding over various activities of the state, one important function was the minting of coins, which was carried out at her temple. To honor this aspect of Juno, place pieces of green aventurine, green calcite, pearls, or staurolite on your altar for the day. Also use these crystals in a money spell to call on her power for financial success.

THROW JEALOUSY AWAY

Although we don't like to admit it, jealousy is a feeling that may nip at our heels from time to time. For help, you will need two pieces of sugilite. Write a few keywords on a small piece of paper about what or who is the source of your jealousy, and then roll the paper into a ball. Hold this ball in your hands along with one piece of sugilite as you visualize these feelings being drawn away by the stone. Set the stone aside and throw the paper away. Hold the other piece of sugilite for a few minutes to help balance your emotions.

ENHANCE MEDITATION AND ASTRAL WORK

Hold a piece of cerussite or keep it in your pocket during meditation or astral travel. Even the most unassuming cerussite crystal is a powerhouse of energy. It aids in reaching new levels of consciousness while meditating and helps to expand awareness during astral travel. This crystal brings clarity to and aids in understanding information we may receive during these practices. Cerussite also helps to ground and center energy afterward.

• • •

Cerussite was carved for ornamental objects in Babylon and Turkey. The Egyptians crushed it and used it mainly for cosmetics. Today, cerussite is popular for its intricate twinning crystals that often form V-shaped chevrons or multiple crystals that form sixlings.

JUNE 4
TRUST YOUR INSTINCTS

We sometimes second-guess our hunches because we don't always trust our innate wisdom or intuition. Before ruling out your initial assessment of a situation or person, take time to let your inner voice be heard. Close your eyes and hold a piece of red spinel to your forehead for a minute or two. Let its energy guide you to the insight and truth you possess. This is also an effective method for developing and strengthening intuition.

— • • • —

Red spinel was originally thought to be a type of ruby
because of its resemblance to that stone and the fact
that it is often found with rubies and sapphires.

AWAKEN SEXUAL ENERGY

Usually depicted as a coiled snake at the base of the spine, kundalini energy can enhance sexuality. To awaken and activate this energy, hold a piece of snakeskin agate against your lower back as you visualize the energy uncoiling at the base of your spine. When this energy moves, it splits into two channels that wind back and forth as it travels up along the spine. Visualize this energy as it moves up your back, and then throughout your body. Take a few minutes to rest after your visualization, and then place the crystal under your bed.

GIVE A TREE A BOOST

In addition to using organic gardening methods to help your plants flourish, call on the energy of tree agate to enhance the health and growth of the trees and shrubs in your yard. Place a stone in each of the cardinal directions around the base of each tree or bush. As you position the crystals say:

Blessings to you, beautiful tree.
Love and light, blessed be.

Leave the stones in place all summer, and then gather them in after the leaves have fallen.

CELEBRATE VESTA

The Roman celebration of *Vestalia* occurred around this time of year and lasted nine days. It began with a ceremony called the *Vesta Aperit*, "the opening" (Salzman 1990, 160). This referred to the inner sanctuary of Vesta's temple and the special occasion when women other than her priestesses could take part in ritual in this most sacred of spaces. Use chrysoprase on your altar to honor Vesta, the goddess of hearth and home. Also, include this stone in women's rituals to focus and boost the energy.

• • •

Worshipped in every household of ancient Rome,
another important function of Vesta
was to protect and save innocents from danger.
Priestesses in her temples were known as Vestal Virgins.

GROUND THAT NEGATIVITY

From time to time, we can feel dogged by negative energy without a clue as to where it is coming from. For protection against this type of situation, place a piece of andalusite in a sachet to use as a charm or wear this stone in a piece of jewelry. Strongly associated with the element earth, andalusite is a grounding force for dealing with all forms of negativity, even if you do not know its source.

• • •

Andalusite was named for Andalusia, the province in Spain where it was discovered. Nicknamed poor man's alexandrite, transparent stones are strongly dichroic, presenting two colors similar to alexandrite when viewed from different angles.

JUNE 9
SET ASIDE SHYNESS

Shyness can sometimes hold us back from what we want to do or achieve. For a little help in overcoming it, hold a piece of apatite as you think of the types of situations in which you feel shy. Let your feelings flow into the stone, and then put the crystal in an envelope. As you do this say:

Apatite, be my guide
as I set these feelings aside.
Shyness is no longer for me,
this I swear, so mote it be.

Place the envelope in the back of a closet or drawer where you can ignore shyness and move on.

THE CELTIC OGHAM DUIR, MONTH OF OAK BEGINS

This Ogham ushers in a period of wisdom with an emphasis on inner strength, endurance, and truth. With strength comes confidence, which makes this a good time to work on self-confidence. The message Duir brings is to keep moving forward. Great opportunities will come your way no matter how small they may seem at first as long as you hang in there. Use white quartz, chrysoberyl, or dioptase to draw on the power of this Ogham.

Figure 16: The Ogham Duir

JUNE 11
BREAK THROUGH BARRIERS

Sometimes particular situations can feel like barriers that keep us from getting what we want or doing what we want to do. Instead of seeing your situation as a barrier, view it as a challenge and overcome it with a little magic. Write a few keywords related to your situation on a small piece of paper. Put it on a shelf and place a piece of lodestone on top of it as you visualize the stone reducing the size of your challenge. Once the situation is resolved, safely burn the paper and scatter the ashes outside.

• • •

Also known as magnetite, the magnetic properties of lodestone were noted by the ancient Greeks. During medieval times, a compass was believed to point north because of an attraction to the North Star, which came to be known as the Lodestar.

BOOST PSYCHIC AWARENESS

Before a divination session or any practice involving psychic abilities, hold a piece of calcite between your palms for several minutes. When the energy of the stone seems to vibrate, place it against your third eye chakra—located slightly above and between your eyebrows. When you feel the chakra vibrate, hold the stone against the top of your head to open your crown chakra. Activating these chakras supports receptivity and intuition. Sit quietly for a moment or two, and then continue with your practice.

• • •

*The Mesopotamians, Phoenicians, and Egyptians
used calcite to carve a range of sacred and secular objects.
Known for its well-formed crystals, today it is a popular
and widely collected mineral. Along with quartz,
it is one of the most common minerals on Earth.*

Use the energy of sunstone to celebrate the long days and warm weather of this month. Make a circle on your altar with pieces of sunstone. As you put each crystal in place, say:

Shining sun, our daystar bright,
fill this stone with your glorious light.

Later, use these stones to power your magic work and rituals with the energy of the sun. On rainy days, place them on a windowsill or on your desk at work to brighten the energy of a room.

JUNE 14

THE RUNIC HALF MONTH OF DAGAZ BEGINS

Starting just before the summer solstice, the period of the Dagaz rune is associated with light, growth, and transformation. Although Dagaz is a rune of change and cycles, it also brings stability and provides a platform upon which we can build something new. Use amethyst, azurite, and kyanite to draw on the power of this rune. These stones are especially effective with this rune when you want to initiate major changes in your life.

Figure 17: The rune Dagaz

JUNE 15
THE VESTA CLUDITUR

Following nine days after the *Vesta Aperit*, this event marked the end of the *Vestalia* celebrations in Rome when the temple of Vesta was closed to the public. The temple was then cleaned and purified. Use this as a special day to purify your crystals. Burn dried lavender flowers in your cauldron, and then pass the crystals through the smoke. Also, waft the smoke around your ritual space to sanctify it.

• • •

It is most appropriate to burn herbs or incense
for cleansing today since Vesta was the Roman goddess of fire.

WARD OFF DANGER

If you are feeling vulnerable because of a particular circumstance or situation, use sard or black agate with white veining in a spell to ward off danger and negativity. Carrying one of these stones in your pocket or wearing it in a piece of jewelry is also effective as a personal energy shield. However, it is important to keep in mind that raising energy to repel danger is not a license to discard common sense.

• • •

Black agate with white, spidery veining opens psychic channels to keep the mind alert. It was used as a talisman during medieval times to guard against danger.

JUNE 17
GAIN CLARITY AND INSIGHT

While developing psychic abilities takes work, we can use certain crystals to boost our learning curve and strengthen our skills. Hold a piece of clear calcite or hawk's-eye between your hands for a moment or two before engaging in psychic practices. Keep the stone with you during the session to gain clarity and insight. In addition, clear quartz is instrumental for dreamwork and hawk's-eye aids in psychic work with animals.

BOOST ENCOURAGEMENT

While your words and actions are the best signs of support when giving someone encouragement, using a crystal can provide an added lift. Yellow zircon is a good choice to amplify and focus your sentiments toward the other person. This crystal also helps to foster happiness and peace. If the person you want to encourage lives with you, place pieces of yellow zircon around the house to surround him or her with encouraging energy. Also consider giving this crystal as a gift.

• • •

Jargon and jargoon are old names for yellow zircon that were derived from the Arabic zarqun meaning "golden color" (Rapp 2002, 104). This stone was widely used for jewelry and ornamental objects during the seventeenth and eighteenth centuries.

Although Minerva's main celebration takes place in March, the Romans also honored this goddess of wisdom in June. Minerva was also the goddess of commerce and the arts. Place pieces of amethyst, pink beryl, or tanzanite zoisite on your altar to show respect for her and to call on her help for spells. These crystals can also be used to call on her for guidance. In addition, use amethyst in a spell to ask for her protection.

RELEASE TOXIC EMOTIONS

To help release negative emotions, hold a couple of pieces of peridot in your hands and close your eyes. Because peridot is usually formed from volcanic activity, visualize the stones shooting a column of energy out of the top of your head as they burn away any toxic or upsetting feelings. Let the image slowly fade away as you bring your attention back to where you are standing or sitting. The warming qualities of peridot will replace the negativity with happiness and harmony. It will also help to instill a sense of peace.

———— • • • ————

In the past, peridot was sometimes called evening emerald because it maintained its color and did not darken as the sunlight faded. It became popular in northern Europe when Christian crusaders took it home with them from their travels in the Middle East.

CONNECT WITH PLANT SPIRITS

Now that gardens are well into their growth cycles, it is easier to connect with the spirits that inhabit plants. Sit or kneel next to a plant. Hold several pieces of amber, jade, and/or labradorite against your heart to open your energy and let it flow into the stones. Make a circle around the base of the plant with the stones, and then place your palms near the leaves or flowers as you visualize your energy connecting with the plant. Pay careful attention for energy coming back to you. Afterward, leave a couple of the crystals as offerings.

LITHA, THE SUMMER SOLSTICE

Summer solstice falls midway between the two equinoxes and marks the longest day of the year when the sun reaches its farthest point north. It is a celebration of the Goddess in her full aspect as mother and the God who is at his pinnacle of power. It is a celebration of light and life. Crystals for your altar or magic work that support the energy of this sabbat include amber, citrine, diamond, emerald, jade, lapis lazuli, sunstone, and tiger's-eye.

Cancer brings a period of nurturing that focuses on the family and home as well as protection. It fosters and supports psychic abilities and provides an opportunity to use your sensitivity to develop intuition. This is also a time of fertility that encompasses procreation and creativity. Crystals that are especially effective to draw on the power of this sun sign include agate, carnelian, emerald, moonstone, pearl, rose quartz, sapphire, selenite, and red zircon. Amber, beryl, calcite, and ruby are also associated with this constellation. In the past, sapphire was considered especially lucky for people born under this sign.

JUNE 23
MIDSUMMER'S EVE

Up until the eighteenth century in rural England, it was customary to light bonfires on hilltops on this night to celebrate the long summer days. When the fires died down, people would leap over them or lead their cattle or sheep between two fires for the symbolic purification of smoke. This is a good time to burn herbs or incense and pass your gemstones through the smoke to cleanse their energy and tap into the magic of Midsummer's Eve.

• • •

Particularly good herbs to use to cleanse crystals on Midsummer's Eve include chamomile, heather, lavender, St. John's wort, and vervain.

JUNE 24
WHERE TO GO FOR VACATION

Summer usually brings a time for travel. However, with so many options, it can be difficult to make up our minds. Place a piece of aventurine under your pillow or on your bedside table to help give you confidence in making a decision. Take the crystal with you when you travel. Aventurine is also a stone of opportunities so don't be surprised if you have some wonderfully serendipitous experiences wherever your summer travel takes you.

• • •

Aventurine is a type of quartz in which tiny inclusions create a sheen of glittering reflections called aventurescence. This mineral takes its name from the famous aventurine glass of Italy, which was accidentally created when copper filings were spilled into molten glass.

DRAW DOWN THE STARS

Since ancient times, the beauty of the night sky has mesmerized people. On a warm summer night, we can't help but feel the awesome power of the stars when we stand outside under the celestial canopy. Hold a piece of celestine as you gaze at the sky to help you draw on the energy and wisdom of a particular star or constellation. Afterward, use this crystal to boost the power of a ritual or spell.

● ● ●

The name of this stone comes from the Latin caelestis *meaning "celestial," which is quite appropriate for its ethereal quality (Oldershaw 2003, 82). Celestine is associated with the element air and the goddess Athena.*

Every now and then, we come to the realization that we need to make changes and let go of certain things in our lives. This could be an object, habit, or situation. Use your birthstone to represent you and a piece of carnelian to represent what you want to release. Place the stones about three inches apart on your altar. Put a piece of moldavite between the stones. Visualize the moldavite initiating the release and your attachment dissolving. Leave the stones in place until you feel that you are ready to move on.

JUNE 27

NO TIME FOR STRESS

Although we spend months looking forward to summer fun, the season can bring some challenges when it arrives. If this happens, lepidolite or smithsonite can come to the rescue with calming energy that relieves stress. Keep a piece of either stone handy at home, work, and in your car so you can be ready for any situation. When you feel frazzled, take a little time out to hold the stone and visualize your tension draining away.

• • •

Lepidolite is usually colorless, pale lilac, pale pink, or white, and occasionally gray or yellowish. It is mottled or veined and often has sparkles from tiny flecks of mica. In the past, it was called lilac stone because that was a favored color.

JUNE 28
BIND A PLEDGE

Whether you make a pledge to yourself or someone else, increase its strength by binding it in fire. Write your pledge on a piece of paper, and then wrap it around a piece of sard. Hold the paper and stone bundle between your hands as you repeat your pledge. Place the bundle in your cauldron and burn the paper. After it cools, remove the stone and scatter the ashes outside. Put the piece of sard in a place where you will see it often and be reminded of your pledge.

THE RUNIC HALF MONTH OF FEHU BEGINS

The rune Fehu is associated with wealth and prosperity, especially portable wealth or liquid assets. More importantly, the underlying energy of this period is concerned with the power to attain and hold on to prosperity. It also relates to having enough control over your life to be independent and self-reliant. Spells for abundance, prosperity, and success at this time can get a boost from this rune. Aventurine or green and pink tourmaline are effective crystals for tapping into the energy of Fehu.

Figure 18: The rune Fehu

JUNE 30
NEVER STOP LEARNING

School may be out for summer but that does not mean you should stop learning and using your mind for critical thinking. Sphene is a stone that fosters mental power and provides encouragement to expand knowledge. Yellow beryl is another crystal that supports the enjoyment of learning. Keep both of these crystals in areas of your home where you will see them often and be encouraged to learn something new. If you are attending a summer class, take these crystals with you for support.

• • •

Yellow beryl ranges from golden to greenish yellow and is also known as heliodor. The name comes from the Greek helios *and* doron *meaning "gift from the sun" (Schumann 2006, 112).*

NOTES

_____

_____

_____

_____

_____

_____

_____

_____

_____

_____

_____

_____

_____

_____

_____

_____

_____

_____

_____

CHAPTER 8

JULY

This month brings us into high summer, a time to bask in the sun and take time to relax. It's a time to take a break from ordinary routines. Brilliant as little suns but cool as an evening breeze, crystals embody the fun and magic of summer.

JULY BIRTHSTONES

American: ruby (traditional), turquoise

British: carnelian (alternate), onyx (alternate), ruby

Others: jade, rubellite (a variety of pink/red tourmaline), sardonyx, spinel

European fifteenth to twentieth century: onyx, turquoise

THIS MONTH'S FULL MOON

The full moon of July is known as the Blessing Moon, Wort (Herb) Moon, Mead Moon, and Thunder Moon. As we enjoy the blessings of summer, this moon is conducive to deeply meaningful dreamwork. It also provides an opportunity for especially strong magic. In addition, it is conducive for meditating on your path and purpose in life. Crystals that are particularly effective with the energy of this moon include carnelian, hematite, malachite, onyx, sapphire, and spinel. Ruby, red tourmaline, and turquoise are also associated with it.

JULY 1
CAPTURE THE SUMMER SUN

Even though the summer solstice has passed, the days are still long and bright. As you enjoy this season, capture some solar energy for magic work. Place a few pieces of yellow beryl, red or orange calcite, Herkimer diamond, and/or sunstone outside for a few hours. When you take them indoors, wrap them individually in pieces of yellow cloth until you need their energy for spells or ritual. Also, consider saving one for your Yule altar in December.

• • •

Herkimer diamond is neither a unique species of mineral, nor a diamond. It is the name given to doubly terminated, gem-quality clear quartz crystals found in Herkimer County, New York. Although it is found in other places, only the ones from Herkimer County can claim this name.

Cleaning house and donating things is a good way to get rid of the items we no longer need. In addition to passing along feelings of goodwill, send a little magic and good vibes. Hold a piece of fluorite as you say three times:

May these things that have been mine
find good use one more time.
May they carry peace and goodwill;
and someone's dream help fulfill.

Place the stone in the bottom of the box or bag before packing the items.

JULY 3
SLEEP WELL

With long daylight hours and so much activity, it may be a challenge to get enough sleep. If this happens, let the energy of blue topaz help you. Sit on the edge of your bed holding the crystal, close your eyes, and take a long, slow breath. Take a moment or two to visualize the stone surrounding you in comforting, blue light. Afterward, place the crystal on your bedside table or in a sachet that can be hung from a bedpost. This stone's calming energy enhances sleep and guards against nightmares.

• • •

This variety of topaz is pale blue or sometimes a light greenish blue that can be mistaken for aquamarine. Blue topaz is weakly dichroic, appearing light or dark blue from different angles. It is associated with the elements air and water.

CELEBRATE YOUR INDEPENDENCE

Independence takes many forms. Whether you want to celebrate the American holiday or your personal independence, wear aquamarine, green aventurine, jade, or tourmaline. Alternatively, place several of these stones around your home where they will be a visible reminder of your independence or spend some time in contemplation of what it means to you. Of course, you could also just go with the colors red, white, and blue to mark the holiday.

JULY 5

HONOR MOTHER GODDESSES

In this time of fullness with blooming flowers and ripening crops, celebrate and honor the earth and all mother goddesses. Place pieces of brown agate, andalusite, chrysoprase, diopside, and/or moss agate around your home or on an outdoor altar in your garden as you give thanks for the abundance and beauty of summer. Extend the range of your acknowledgment by taking a walk or hike and leaving a stone in some of your favorite places along the way.

— • • • —

Chrysoprase has been prized as a gem since ancient times.
The Greeks, Romans, and Egyptians used it for jewelry
and ornamental objects. In Egyptian jewelry,
it was often set with lapis lazuli.

ADAPT TO A SUMMER SCHEDULE

With summer travel and children out of school, our daily schedules have to be rearranged and the rhythm of our lives is disrupted. Although the change is pleasant, we sometimes need a little help adjusting to the new routine. Staurolite is just the crystal to help us find smooth sailing into summer. Wear this stone in jewelry or carry it with you when traveling. Also, place pieces of staurolite around your home to help you take everything in stride.

———— • • • ————

Intergrown twin crystals of staurolite frequently form two types of crosses. In one, the crystals cross at a ninety-degree angle and in the other they cross at sixty degrees, forming an X shape. Although rare, three crystals growing together can form a starlike shape.

HALT AGGRESSION

If you work with people who tend to be aggressive, keep several pieces of obsidian in your workspace. Before taking the stones to work, cleanse them in the smoke of mugwort as you say:

> *Black stone, like a mirror shine,*
> *help resolve this problem of mine.*
> *When aggressive vibes come my way,*
> *bounce them back, keep them away.*

Position the stones in several places on or in your desk and around your workspace.

Although we associate holly with Yule, summer is the time of year when this plant comes into bloom. The energy during this time is associated with hearth and home. The Ogham Tinne is also associated with protection. To call on the power of Tinne, draw the Ogham on a picture of a holly leaf and place it on your altar. Position a piece of smoky quartz, citrine, or zoisite on top of the picture and allow it to stay in place until next month when energy is influenced by another Ogham.

Figure 19: The Ogham Tinne

JULY 9
ADD ENCHANTMENT
TO YOUR SUMMER MAGIC

With a soft glow like moonlight, selenite adds lunar power and enchantment to spells and rituals, especially when performed outdoors in the summer. In addition, this stone provides inspiration for choosing the right words for your magic. Place a piece of selenite on your altar or use four of them to define the cardinal directions. Selenite will also keep negative energy at bay during ritual or spellwork. The best way to prepare a selenite crystal for this is to simply sit with it in the moonlight and let Luna bestow her magic and blessings.

DEEPEN LOVE

A romantic relationship is always nice, but when you and your partner are ready to move deeper, rhodonite can open the way. The complex veining pattern of this stone symbolizes the intertwining energy, love, and devotion of two people drawing their lives together. Give your beloved a piece of jewelry or other special object made from rhodonite. As a stone of peace, this crystal attracts happiness to the home and relationships.

• • •

Although its name and colors are similar to rhodochrosite, rhodonite can be distinguished by its black veining that forms weblike patterns. Rhodonite is usually mottled with rose pink to dark red or orange red.

JULY 11
BUCKLE DOWN AND WORK

It usually starts with spring fever and by the time summer arrives, focusing on a job or necessary tasks—when we would rather be outside relaxing or playing—can be difficult. The mineral fluorite can rescue this situation. This crystal enhances concentration and mental power and helps us stay on track. Place a couple of pieces of fluorite on your desk to motivate you toward a more analytical mind-set. Also, keep a stone with you in meetings to keep discussions focused.

SEE OR HEAR BEYOND

If you think that you may have clairvoyant or clairaudient abilities, the crystal apatite can help you. This stone is instrumental in developing and fine-tuning these psychic skills. Before a practice session, hold a piece of apatite in each hand while you sit quietly for a few minutes as your energy attunes to the stones. Keep in mind that the stones are only an aid and you will need to work at these talents on a regular basis. In addition to psychic abilities, apatite enhances communication on all levels.

• • •

Apatite can be blue, colorless, green, pink, violet, or yellow.
It may exhibit a cat's-eye effect when cut
in a smooth dome shape.
Apatite is associated with the
elements air, earth, and fire.

JULY 13
HAPPY BIRTHDAY, JOHN DEE

Born on this day in 1527, John Dee was an astronomer, mathematician, and advisor to England's Queen Elizabeth I (Clucas 2006, 347). Dee is still well known today as an astrologer and occult philosopher. To honor him, place pieces of beryl, obsidian, or clear quartz on your altar. Dee was known to have used these types of crystals for scrying. You might also want to use these crystals for scrying or working a little magic today.

Symbolizing strength and the vitality of life, the Uruz runic half month is a period of high energy and action. In addition, Uruz is an aid for maintaining well-being and raising energy for healing. The power of this rune can be employed to manifest what you personally seek in relation to these aspects and to help others. Use jasper or sunstone with hematite or lepidolite to work with the energy of Uruz.

Figure 20: The rune Uruz

GETTING TO KNOW YOURSELF

With so many things to keep track of in our lives, we often focus on everyone else in the family or friends and lose touch with our inner selves. When this happens, take time for introspection by sitting quietly while holding a piece of blue tourmaline. This stone aids in bringing clarity and insight for accessing self-knowledge. Keep it in a place where you will see it often and be reminded to keep in touch with yourself.

———— • • • ————

Blue tourmaline is also known as indicolite and indigolite. It can be deep blue or neon blue and many shades in between. It is strongly dichroic, appearing light blue and dark blue from different angles.

HEIGHTEN YOUR SENSES

Spending more time outdoors in the summer means that there are so many sensations to experience and enjoy. Carry a piece of rainbow obsidian to heighten your awareness and senses so you can fully engage with the natural world. Acting as a filter, this crystal is a discerning stone that will keep you from feeling overloaded by too much input. Rainbow obsidian is particularly supportive when performing rituals outside.

• • •

*This variety of obsidian has flowing bands
of iridescent colors created by inclusions within the stone.
These inclusions produce a unique effect depending
on the angle from which the stone is viewed.*

PREPARE TO CONTACT SPIRITS

The aura—an energy field around the body—is an important tool for contacting spirits and for working in the spirit realm. Keeping our energy receptive heightens the experience. Before embarking on spirit-related practices, use a piece of labradorite to "comb" your aura. Starting above your head, move the stone as though it were a comb passing through the energy around your body. When you get to your feet, comb the energy outward and away from you, which will carry away any negativity.

If you feel that you need protection from a hex, use four long, clear quartz crystals to build defense. Place them on your altar with each point facing one of the cardinal directions. As you position them say:

Crystal of quartz, strong and clear,
keep all hexes from coming near.
Guard this house and all within;
no time to waste, let it begin.

Allow the crystals to remain in place for as long as you feel it is necessary.

JULY 19
MANIFEST YOUR DREAMS

Effective dreamwork takes a little preparation. Before going to bed, hold a piece of hematite for a few minutes as you think of the good things you want to draw into your life. As you do this, say:

> *Dark stone hematite,*
> *listen to my dreams tonight.*
> *May these good things come to me,*
> *with your help, so mote it be.*

Leave the stone on your bedside table overnight, and then carry it with you the following day.

JULY 20
KISS AND MAKE UP

Unfortunately, we sometimes say things that cause a disagreement or quarrel with a partner. For help in making up, wear a piece of lodestone jewelry. When you put it on, visualize the stone functioning as a white flag to signal a truce. This mineral is a stone of forgiveness that is especially helpful in reconciling a marriage or other very close relationship. Lodestone will also help to strengthen feelings of loyalty.

— • • • —

In China, lodestone was called the loving stone because its magnetic properties represented the powers of attraction.

JULY 21
DARK MOON MAGIC

You will most likely need to swap this entry with the one that falls on the actual date of the new/dark moon in this month. Go outside or stand at a window to draw down the energy of the moon into an opal or clear quartz crystal. Both of these stones are instrumental for stimulating cosmic awareness. Wrap the stone in a black cloth until you need it to enhance astral work or strengthen a spell.

• • •

The special optical effect called opalescence
gives many common opals a slightly
milky-blue appearance that echoes the beauty of the moon.

JULY 22
SAY GOOD-BYE TO LONELINESS

Whether or not we may realize it, loneliness is something we can change. It begins by opening our energy and being receptive to friendship. Hold a piece of rose quartz and visualize a soft, pink light surrounding you and extending outward. Take note of any sensation that occurs, and then recall it when you are around people with whom you would like to be friends. It also helps to wear rose quartz jewelry or to carry a piece in your pocket.

• • •

The energy of pink stones works directly with the heart
to gently open the soul and psyche
to receive healing and goodness.
To softly amplify the power of a pink crystal,
put a tiny dab of geranium, lavender,
or palmarosa essential oil on it.

THE ZODIAC CHANGES TO LEO

The lion symbolizes strength, power, leadership, and authority. This is a time to foster these qualities, but it must be done with integrity and care in order to avoid inflated pride and ambition. A true lion is a guardian that provides protection and guidance. Gemstones that are particularly effective for working with the power of Leo include amber, yellow beryl, carnelian, citrine, danburite, jasper, kunzite, labradorite, peridot, rhodochrosite, ruby, sardonyx, sunstone, and tiger's-eye. Other crystals associated with this sign include chrysoberyl, garnet, topaz, and zircon. In the past, diamond was considered especially lucky for people born under this sign.

JULY 24
OUTDOOR PSYCHIC WORK

With warm, inviting weather, most of us spend as much time as we can outdoors during the summer. It is also conducive for psychic practices, which are enhanced by the close proximity to nature. Azurite is an effective stone for warding off any negativity to which you may be exposed when you engage in these activities outside. In addition, this crystal is especially supportive for clairvoyance and all forms of divination.

JULY 25
GO FULL TILT
OR REIN IN PASSION

Sometimes we need help to stoke our passions—both amorous and creative. At other times, we can get carried away with these passions and may need a little help to tone down our enthusiasm. Red spinel helps in both circumstances to raise or ratchet down the energy and keep these passions in balance. Hold this crystal and mindfully visualize which direction you want its energy to take you.

• • •

Like ruby, red spinel fluoresces in daylight,
making it look like a smoldering ember.
Because of the confusion about these stones,
several famous rubies, including some in the British
crown jewels, are actually red spinel.

JULY 26

FOSTER PROTECTION AND LOVE IN YOUR HOME

Hold a piece of red agate between your hands as you send loving energy into it. Afterward, use this stone to build protective energy around your home. Touch it to each exterior wall—or interior wall if you live in an apartment—as you say:

Stone of red, may your energy spread
around each wall, encompassing all.
From ceiling to floor,
safe and secure.

Keep this crystal in the kitchen or whichever room is the heart of your home.

STRENGTHEN WILLPOWER

To boost a spell, use a piece of pyrite when you prepare for it. On the night before, place the stone with the things you plan to use for the spell. Alternatively, write your intentions on a piece of paper, and then wrap it around the stone. Pyrite strengthens willpower and aids in manifesting intentions and dreams. This stone is also effective in keeping energy grounded during magic work, which makes it helpful after spellwork and rituals, too.

———— • • • ————

During the Middle Ages,
pyrite was known as marcasite,
the name of a similar mineral.
While the real marcasite has
the same chemical composition as pyrite,
it has a different crystal structure.
Pyrite was popular in Victorian times,
but it was still wrongly called marcasite.

JULY 28

COSMIC ENERGY
FOR TRANSFORMATION

Starting in mid-July, the Delta Aquarid meteor showers peak late in the month. Use a piece of moldavite to tap into this cosmic energy to aid in personal transformation. Moldavite is a tektite, which is a rock that was formed from the melting and rapid cooling of terrestrial rocks that were vaporized by the high-energy impacts of meteorites. Go outside and hold the stone up toward the sky as you say three times:

> *Moldavite, stone of power and might,*
> *hold cosmic energy for me tonight.*

When you go indoors, hold the stone as you meditate on the transformation you seek.

THE RUNIC HALF MONTH OF THURISAZ BEGINS

Marking a time for initiating changes and quests, the rune Thurisaz brings in a period for developing and strengthening willpower, which is instrumental when making major changes. Thurisaz also aids in spells for protection and defense. Paint this rune on a crystal to draw on the energy of Thurisaz for any of these endeavors. While citrine is the best stone to use when working with the energy of this rune, lepidolite with rutilated quartz or tourmalated quartz also works well.

Figure 21: The rune Thurisaz

WORK WITH ANGELS

Although angels often reach out to us, even when we are aware of it we sometimes need a little help in communicating with them. Both angelite and barite are powerful crystals that can help you tune into the presence of angels. These stones also aid in understanding messages you may receive from them or from other spirit beings. Hold a piece of angelite or barite, or place it on your altar when engaging in this work.

JULY 31
CHANNEL YOUR SENSITIVITY

If you are particularly sensitive to the energy around you, you know what a challenge it can be when around other people. Rather than denying or trying to subdue your sensitivity, learn to appreciate your gift of receptiveness. With the help of the crystal cuprite, you can learn to channel your energy and use it for productive empathy to support others in need. This stone is very grounding, which provides emotional protection for you, as well.

───── • • • ─────

*Cuprite is crimson red and sometimes
so dark that it almost appears black.
Cuprite is popular with mineral collectors
because of its cube-shaped crystals and deep red reflections.*

NOTES

CHAPTER 9

AUGUST

This month is a time of hot, lazy days that are frequently offset by dazzling thunderstorms. Let the brilliance of crystals bring extra magic to your summer days and nights.

AUGUST BIRTHSTONES

American: peridot, sardonyx (traditional)

British: peridot, sardonyx (alternate)

Others: alexandrite, aventurine, emerald, jade, onyx, sapphire, tourmaline

European fifteenth to twentieth century: carnelian, moonstone, sardonyx, topaz

THIS MONTH'S FULL MOON

This moon is known as the Barley Moon, Corn Moon, Sturgeon Moon, and Wort (Herb) Moon. As these names suggest, August is a good time to give thought to where our food originates and to show reverence for the cycles that produce it. In addition, this moon is conducive for animal magic and prophecy. Crystals that are especially effective to use during this esbat include carnelian, hawk's-eye, jade, jasper, labradorite, and tiger's-eye. Emerald, moonstone, peridot, and sardonyx are also associated with this moon.

AUGUST 1
LAMMAS, LUGHNASADH

Despite the Gaelic name, *Lughnasadh,* being a reference to the god Lugh, this is not a solar celebration but one associated with the earth. It centers on the major grain harvests when the first loaves of bread are made from fresh-cut grain. This is also a celebration of the seeds that have been gathered for next year's crop. Resembling the colors of grain, citrine, yellow diamond, and peridot embody the energy of this sabbat and its hopeful prospects for the future. Topaz and jasper can also be used.

AUGUST 2
STAY CONNECTED WITH THE NATURAL WORLD

If you live in a city or spend a lot of time indoors, moss or tree agate can help you stay in contact with the energy and rhythm of the natural world. Spend a few minutes each day to hold a piece of either agate between your palms as you visualize your favorite outdoor place. Also, take one of these crystals with you when you go on an excursion. Because the energy of these stones is very grounding, they are especially useful after rituals.

HONOR ATHENA

Taking place around this time of year, the *Panathenaia* was an annual Greek festival that honored Athena, a major goddess of crafts, protection, and wisdom. A larger festival, the Great Panathenaia, was held every four years. To honor Athena, light a yellow candle on your altar and place pieces of celestine and/or obsidian around the base of it. Also, use these stones to call on Athena for help in developing your magical skills or for protection.

• • •

According to myth, Athena won possession of the city of Athens by producing the olive tree, which the citizens deemed more useful than the salt spring Poseidon created. The olive tree became an integral part of Greek culture and cuisine.

FEND OFF BLACK MAGIC

To guard against black magic and provide protection from hexes, use crystals such as jasper, jet, or onyx to boost defensive spells. Afterward, wrap the stone in a black cloth and store it in an out-of-the-way place in your home. In addition, place one of these stones at each corner of your property or house and visualize their energy rising and connecting above the roof, creating a dome of energy around you and your home.

—————— • • • ——————

Confusion about onyx dates to the conflicting information from ancient writers and continues today with the name often used only for completely black stones.
Onyx consists of alternating layers of black and white.

AUGUST 5
THE CELTIC OGHAM COLL, MONTH OF HAZEL BEGINS

The Ogham Coll marks a period that is associated with creativity and inspiration. Also strongly associated with wisdom, this Ogham supports both learning and teaching. It fosters the pursuit of knowledge and offers insight for attaining more than superficial information. This is also a time when esoteric knowledge and great wisdom are more easily accessible. Information received during divination sessions at this time may have a more significant meaning. Use red agate, amethyst, or tiger's-eye to enhance your practices and provide a boost to spells.

Figure 22: The Ogham Coll

BURN AWAY PROBLEMS

Sometimes we think that a problem is bigger than it is, and occasionally we perceive a problem where none exists. For help in getting things into perspective, prepare a piece of fire agate or fire opal by passing it through the smoke of frankincense or dragon's blood incense. As you do this say:

Power of smoke, power of fire,
help me get out of this mire.
Lift this feeling that's holding me,
remove this problem, set me free.

Sit quietly as you hold the stone and briefly review the situation that is troubling you. Visualize the stone setting a spark and your problem burning down to a pile of ash. End your visualization by blowing the ashes away.

AUGUST 7
MAINTAIN DIGNITY

In this rough and tumble world, our self-respect and dignity can take a beating. If this happens, wear or carry a piece of sard to bolster your energy and support your sense of self. When putting the jewelry on or putting the stone in your pocket, stand straight and hold your chin up. Feel your body surrounded by the warm energy of this stone. Sard fosters respect for oneself as well as others.

Regardless of whether or not you can plan a vacation get-away, astral travel can provide an interesting and rewarding experience. When you are ready for your astral journey, lie down and place one piece of moldavite at your head and one at your feet. Afterward, spend a couple of minutes sitting quietly as you hold one of the stones in each hand. Moldavite is associated with cosmic consciousness and can bring meaningful insight about an astral excursion when you return to the mundane world.

── • • • ──

Moldavite is a form of natural glass called a tektite.
Once thought to be of extraterrestrial origin,
tektites are formed from the melting and
rapid cooling of terrestrial rocks that were
vaporized by the high-energy impacts of meteorites.

AUGUST 9
FORGIVE A FRIEND

As in any relationship, we have ups and downs and some-times a falling out with our friends. Occasionally, pride or a simple misunderstanding gets in the way, which can lead us down a negative path that in our heart of hearts we do not want to follow. Use rhodochrosite in spells or meditation to aid you in finding your way clear with forgiveness and com-passion. Keep this stone on your altar or in a special place until things improve.

WEAR PEARLS FOR WISDOM

When you anticipate a challenging meeting or day at work, plan to wear a piece of pearl jewelry or put a loose pearl in your pocket. Beforehand, take the pearl or jewelry to the ocean or make salt water by dissolving a pinch of sea salt in warm water. Dip the pearl(s) in the water as you say three times:

Pearl of guidance and clarity,
bring me wisdom, so mote it be.

This is also helpful when dealing with a family situation.

There are as many theories regarding the origin of the Puck Fair as there are forms of celebration, but in general, it pays tribute to the spirit of the wild. Of course, Shakespeare's Puck was equated with the famous brownie of folklore, Robin Goodfellow. Because of this, I think today is a good time to acknowledge and celebrate the sometimes mischievous wee folk. Leave offerings of jade, clear quartz, and/or staurolite, which will also protect against their pranks.

—— • • • ——

The adventures of Robin Goodfellow were a popular
part of folklore in medieval Britain.
Although only half fairy, he had a penchant for good-humored
trickery. In Robin Hood fashion, his shenanigans helped
the needy at the expense of the well off or pompous.

AUGUST 12
LYCHNAPSIA, CELEBRATE ISIS

The Roman festival called *Lychnapsia* was a celebration to mark the birthday of Isis. To honor this mighty goddess, numerous oil lamps were lit in her temples. Although an Egyptian goddess, the Romans honored Isis as a goddess of the earth, protector of the dead, and patron of loving wives and mothers. Light several candles on your altar and place pieces of carnelian, emerald, jasper, lapis lazuli, moonstone, or star sapphire around them to honor Isis. Also, use these stones to call on her blessings.

• • •

Emeralds were mined in Egypt on the Red Sea coast long before Cleopatra's name was associated with the site. Emeralds are unusual in that their inclusions are like fingerprints, providing information on where a stone originated.

The rune Ansuz marks a period conducive to receiving both blessings and inspiration. It is also a time of communication—giving power to words, finding truth, and interpreting messages. Use clear quartz and both red and blue tourmaline to work with the energy of Ansuz. Clear quartz aids in opening the channels of communication. Red and blue tourmaline aid in finding truth and understanding the meaning of messages you may receive. Serpentine with iolite are also helpful to work with Ansuz.

Figure 23: The rune Ansuz

FOSTER A HAPPY HOME

To foster happiness and peace in your home, you need to get and keep positive energy flowing. Walk slowly through every room in your house with a handful of blue lace agate crystals. As you do this, visualize how energy would move around furniture and other objects. Place a crystal in locations where you feel energy may get stuck. In addition to this crystal's grounding and centering properties, blue lace agate also fosters trust and true friendship.

• • •

Aptly named, blue lace agate has lacy bands or wavy patterns of powder blue and white. Discovered in the middle of the twentieth century, what this stone lacks in history, it makes up for with powerful energy.

AUGUST 15
STAY ALERT

Although we may enter an altered state of consciousness during any form of psychic work or astral travel, wear or keep a piece of smithsonite nearby to help you maintain an alert mind. To enhance and heighten dreamwork, use smithsonite on its own or with a piece of green jasper, which will foster soothing sleep while you dream. Place both stones in a sachet to hang on a bedpost or set them on your bedside table.

AUGUST 16
SUPPORT INTUITION

For whatever reason, we sometimes second-guess ourselves and ignore that little voice inside that gives us advice. Afterward, we often regret doing this. If you find this occurring on a regular basis, spend a little time at least once a week to meditate as you hold a piece of apophyllite. This stone provides supportive energy and aids in learning to trust inner wisdom. Apophyllite also helps to fine-tune intuitive abilities.

———— • • • ————

In the past, apophyllite was called fisheye stone because
it can sometimes have a pearly luster like a fish's eye.
This is apropos where it comes to intuition,
because this crystal is an aid for looking deep within.

AUGUST 17

SUBDUE ANGER

If anger tends to get the better of you, larimar can help you cope. Prepare a piece of larimar by taking a soothing soak in the tub. Hold the stone and visualize a calm feeling settling over you as all your troubles and negative emotions dissolve like a handful of bath salts. Whenever you feel angry, hold the larimar and replay the visualization in your mind as you say:

Larimar, stone of watery blue,
may this feeling, I subdue.
Make this anger drain away;
may light and love fill this day.

August 18

ENCHANT YOUR DREAMS

In addition to dreamwork, we can simply bring a little magic and enchantment to our nightly dreamscapes. To do this, place small pieces of kyanite under the corners of your mattress or on the floor at the corners of your bed. This stone enhances creativity and brings fullness and depth to dreams. The effects may be subtle at first; however, over time you may find a new richness in the imagery your sleeping mind presents.

AUGUST 19
HONOR JUPITER

Held around this time of year, the *Vinalia Rustica* was a rural Roman festival of the grapevine. During this celebration, Jupiter was called upon as a sky god to protect grapevines from storm damage so the harvest would be bountiful in the autumn. Place a piece of topaz on your altar to honor Jupiter and his power. Also, carry or wear topaz as a protective amulet. Alternatively, use this stone in a spell and call on Jupiter to give it a boost.

• • •

The Roman equivalent of Zeus,
Jupiter was a major war and fertility god.
He was worshipped as a god of soldiers
and was called a patron of ironworkers.
He was a protector of youths and of the Roman state.
Oak trees were sacred to him.

AUGUST 20
ATTRACT GOOD THINGS INTO YOUR LIFE

Use yellow jasper in spells to attract positive energy and draw the good things that you want into your life. Clearing the mind and bringing stability, this stone helps to keep a balanced perspective, especially for achieving success. Light a yellow candle on your altar and hold a piece of yellow jasper. Meditate on what you want, and then say three times:

Yellow stone with flowing design,
draw to me what I want to be mine.

AUGUST 21
ACTIVATE PSYCHIC ENERGY

For more effective divination, dreamwork, or other practice, get psychic energy moving beforehand. Roll several small pieces of iolite between your palms as you visualize white light emanating from the stones and surrounding you. Imagine this light and energy as a conduit through which you can draw wisdom. Let the visualization fade, and then go about your planned practice.

• • •

Iolite is the bluish gem-quality variety of the industrial mineral cordierite. Its name comes from the Greek ion, *meaning "violet," and* lithos, *"stone" (Shipley 1993, 136).*

THE ZODIAC CHANGES TO VIRGO

This is a period for using your head and putting your analytical mind to work, especially if you are looking for business or employment success. Virgo helps us handle the necessary details of planning for the future and creating the building blocks for success. In addition, this is a time for nurturing. Crystals that are especially effective to work with the energy of Virgo include amazonite, amethyst, andalusite, apatite, carnelian, chrysocolla, jade, pink jasper, lapis lazuli, sugilite, tsavorite garnet, and turquoise. Aventurine, emerald, lodestone, moss agate, sapphire, and red zircon are also associated with Virgo. In the past, turquoise and zircon were considered especially lucky for people born under this sign.

Spirituality is not just a set of beliefs; it is a dynamic process that evolves over time as we explore and grow. Even though we may occasionally reach a plateau or even falter, this is part of spiritual development. While the path may sometimes seem obscured, crystals can help us find the way. Amethyst, lodestone, and clear quartz aid in spiritual guidance, especially when worn near the heart or held during meditation. These crystals aid in spiritual guidance and growth.

————— • • • —————

*As the most highly valued quartz, amethyst has enjoyed a long
history of popularity that has rarely waned.
From the pharaohs of Egypt to British monarchs,
this gemstone has been used in countless royal jewelry.
In the mid-seventeenth century,
amethyst was as precious as diamond.*

August 24
Heal Heartbreak

Love can be wonderful but sometimes relationships don't work out and we find ourselves emotionally hurt. If this occurs, surround yourself with rose quartz and/or rhodonite at home, at work, and even in your car. Wearing these crystals is especially helpful. The gentle energy of rose quartz and rhodonite brings healing and eventual happiness. When you are ready, these crystals will help open your heart to love again.

AUGUST 25
CELEBRATE ODIN

According to author Nigel Pennick, it was around this time of year that Norse mythology places the end of Odin's nine-day ordeal (Pennick 2001, 100). In legend, this is the point at which he perceived the runes and their wisdom. To call on the power of the runes and to honor this supreme Norse god, place amber, amethyst, carnelian, garnet, moonstone, opal, ruby, sapphire, or topaz on your altar. If you have a set of runes, place them on your altar, too.

• • •

Sapphire and ruby are the two gem-quality
varieties of the mineral corundum.
Initially, sapphire only referred to blue stones.
Today, this name applies to any gem-quality
corundum that is not red.
Colors other than blue are
sometimes called fancy sapphires.

INSPIRE YOUR CREATIVITY

The crystal serpentine can be instrumental in getting your creative energy flowing. Gather enough serpentine stones of similar size so you can arrange them in a curving pattern—think snake. Lay the stones out on your desk or whatever area you use for creative projects. Take a moment to visualize your serpentine snake stirring up the energy around you. Leave it in place for at least a few days to keep things moving.

───── • • • ─────

Serpentine was so named because its coloring often resembles snakeskin. It can be brown, grayish green, green, or yellow. Green serpentine was popular with the ancient Chinese, Olmec, and Maya because of its resemblance to jade, which they were particularly fond of.

Support for Justice

When seeking justice, bloodstone and tourmaline can help, especially in legal matters. Hold one of these stones as you briefly review the situation before attending to any business related to it. Wearing these stones is also helpful. In addition to support, these crystals aid in removing obstacles that may stand in the way of righting a wrong. More importantly, they aid in maintaining a balanced perspective. Tourmaline helps to keep emotions in check, while bloodstone sustains honesty and integrity.

KEEP TO YOUR PURPOSE

It can be discouraging when we have set our minds to a purpose but seem to have trouble working on it. When this happens, create a circle on your altar with pieces of black spinel. Visualize energy moving around this circle and rising to build a cone of energy. Before releasing the energy, say three times:

> *Powerful spinel, stones of black,*
> *remove whatever is holding me back.*
> *Strengthen purpose for me to fulfill;*
> *so mote it be, this is my will.*

Do this three nights in a row.

The rune Raido brings in a period that fosters and supports movement in all aspects of life. Related to travel, his rune marks a time for reaching personal objectives, which may require some form of travel. Pay attention to communication skills, as this is an integral part of achieving the things that you are striving for. While malachite and turquoise are most effective to call on the power of Raido, sapphire and sodalite can also be used.

Figure 24: The rune Raido

When the proverbial clouds seem to gather and darken your day, take a break to sit quietly and hold a piece of lepidolite. Breathe slowly for a few minutes as you visualize warm sunlight breaking through the clouds and shining on you. This stone is an effective aid for adjusting mental perspective and lifting spirits. In addition, the peaceful energy of lepidolite is instrumental for making changes and bringing harmony into your life.

AUGUST 31
REALIGN YOUR ENERGY

If you feel in need of grounding and/or your energy seems out of whack, use six pieces of green tourmaline to get back to an even flow. Lay the stones on the floor where you will lie down so one piece is near the top of your head, one at each foot, and one at each hand. When you lie down, place another piece on your heart. Clear your mind and let the energy of these crystals work their magic.

• • •

The color of this tourmaline
includes various shades of green.
It is dichroic, appearing light green or
yellow green from different angles.
Bright emerald green stones
are often called chrome tourmaline.

NOTES

CHAPTER 10

SEPTEMBER

This month marks a change of pace in our lives as the energy of summer winds down and we look toward autumn. Crystals help us shift gears and stay in balance as the seasons and our schedules change.

September Birthstone

American: lapis lazuli, sapphire (traditional)

British: lapis lazuli (alternate), sapphire

Others: blue spinel, blue tourmaline, iolite, peridot, sardonyx

European fifteenth to twentieth century: chrysolite (in the past, this name was used for chrysoberyl, peridot, and topaz)

This Month's Full Moon

The full moon of September is known as the Barley Moon, Corn Moon, Harvest Moon, and Wine Moon. September is a time of year when fruits and vegetables that grow on vines are harvested. It is a time of manifestation. The energy of this moon centers on the home and is the perfect time for giving thanks. This moon amplifies spells for confidence and protection. Crystals associated with this esbat include carnelian, cat's-eye, iolite, lapis lazuli, rhodochrosite, sard, and blue tourmaline. Peridot, sapphire, and spinel are also associated with it.

SEPTEMBER 1
INCREASE YOUR MAGICAL POWER

Before engaging in spellwork, hold four pieces of amber in your hands. Clearly visualize what you want to accomplish with your spell, and then place a stone on the floor at each corner of your altar. Visualize yellow light emanating from each piece of amber and charging your altar with energy. Go about casting your spell and when you are ready to send out the energy, visualize the yellow light from the stones increasing and boosting your willpower.

— • • • —

Nicknamed the Jurassic gem, amber ranges from pale yellow to brown and reddish brown. It can contain insects, air bubbles, pollen, and other small pieces of debris. Radial cracks called sun spangles are artificially created by heating a piece of amber.

This period of time is associated with inner growth and energy. Like a vine, our paths do not usually take a straight course; however, if we pay attention, we can learn from the twists and turns that our lives may take. Lay out pieces of amethyst or jasper on your altar in a winding, spiraling vine pattern to draw on the power of Muin for guidance. Like a vine, the energy of Muin can be restrictive, making this an ideal time for binding spells.

Figure 25: The Ogham Muin

GOOD-BYE TO SUMMER

September is a month of changes for the natural world and for our daily routines as we shift from summer into autumn. As a stone of memory and change, andalusite offers assistance during this time of transition. Place a piece of andalusite on a windowsill for a few days where it will catch the sun and remind you of summer. After that, carry the stone with you to provide energetic and grounding support.

• • •

Andalusite can be various shades of brown with a greenish, orange, brown, or yellowish tinge. It can also be gray, pink, white, yellow, or yellow green. Transparent green andalusite is regarded as a top-quality gem.

DOUBLE YOUR LUCK WITH MONEY

With a high copper content, malachite is an especially good stone to power the energy of money spells. It is also associated with fostering luck with money. Place a small mirror on your altar. Hold a piece of malachite and say:

Stone of green, malachite,
hear the wish I make tonight.

Place the stone on the mirror and then say:

As this stone becomes two,
may this wish soon come true.

If you have a nagging feeling that someone has deceived you, use a crystal to open the gates of your intuition. Hold a piece of pyrite in each hand as you visualize the person's face. Listen for your inner voice to help you find the truth and sort out the situation. If a confirmation is not clear, pyrite can provide protection from deceit. Keep a piece of pyrite with you when you are in the presence of the person in question.

· · ·

While it hurts to discover that someone has lied, brassy yellow pyrite can provide an emotional lift and help you let go of the situation.

SEPTEMBER 6
SET YOUR MIND

Spells are more than an intention or wish; they depend on willpower to achieve success. The best way to strengthen your spells is to set your mind to your purpose. By staying determined, your willpower becomes a conduit to manifest the goal you seek. Before engaging in spellwork, hold a piece of tanzanite zoisite against your forehead and draw its energy into your mind. This stone also boosts psychic abilities, which may aid your magic work.

— • • • —

*Also known as blue zoisite, the color of tanzanite
ranges from lilac to sapphire blue to violet.
It is strongly trichroic, appearing in hues of purple,
blue, or brownish yellow from different angles.*

FRESH START BACK TO SCHOOL

Like the beginning of the year in January, a new school year is full of promise, excitement, and potential. Whether you have school-aged children, you yourself are going back to school, or you are simply taking one class, approach it with optimism and zest. Place a piece or two of moss agate and/or chrysoberyl near your front door to send everyone in the family off to school with positive energy.

SEPTEMBER 8
ENCHANT YOUR MORNING

To brighten and bring a magical quality to your morning, hang clear quartz pendants in a window that gets direct sunlight. As they catch the light, they create a sparkling rainbow of colors around the room. Gently tap the pendants so they sway and make the colors dance. Of course, if you don't have a window that gets sun in the morning you can do this to enchant your afternoon.

• • •

As light passes through transparent gemstones,
it can be deflected or refracted at various angles
depending on its internal crystal structure.
This can also make a stone appear extra sparkly.

Nine is considered a magical number because it is a triple of the sacred number three. The ninth day of the ninth month brings a doubling of this threefold magical power. You can harness this energy for spellwork by laying out a square grid of nine crystals on your altar. Use black agate, bloodstone, and rhodonite to create the grid. All of these stones are particularly good for boosting the energy of spells. In addition, black agate sparks creativity; bloodstone is effective for attracting luck, success, and money; and rhodonite attracts love.

September 10
Build a Psychic Shield

When engaging in psychic work, it can be helpful to keep unwanted energy from interfering. Although calcite is a common mineral, it is a powerhouse for psychic protection. Create a circle with pieces of calcite on the floor around you or place the crystals at various points in the room where you are doing any type of psychic work. This stone also provides supportive energy for astral work and divination. In addition, calcite is especially helpful when developing psychic skills.

———— • • • ————

When we make a circle,
we are creating a very special and powerful space—
a space where our energies become focused and strengthened;
a space where we share in the mysteries of body, mind,
and spirit, of time and eternity.

SEPTEMBER 11
HOLD A SECRET

When a friend shares information in confidence, we are bound by loyalty to hold our tongues. Occasionally it may be difficult to keep a secret, but if this happens, you can turn to green garnet for help. This crystal is associated with loyalty and fidelity in relationships. Paint your friend's initials on the stone as you say:

Let this stone be a cue;
to my friend, I remain true.

Carry it with you or leave it on your altar.

SEPTEMBER 12
ALL YOU NEED IS LOVE

Love is a wonderful and powerful feeling, but you don't have to be in love with someone to experience it. Crystals help us tap into the energy of universal love and draw it into our lives. Keep pieces of calcite or sugilite in your home, car, and workplace to surround yourself with this energy. These stones also foster a sense of well-being and aid in spiritual growth. If you have a garden, place a couple crystals outside to extend the energy of love around your property.

• • •

*Sugilite ranges from deep purple to lavender
and violet to reddish violet.
Crystals of lighter shades of lavender
have been called lavulite.
The spelling is sometimes altered to luvulite
to emphasize its association with love (luv).*

This half month of Kaunaz focuses on the type of knowledge that illuminates and enlightens us. It is a time for finding clarity and for igniting creativity. To aid you in this, arrange pieces of amber or blue tourmaline in the shape of this rune on your altar. Opal and jade together also work well with this rune. Let the energy of these stones kindle deep knowledge and spark your imagination.

Figure 26: The rune Kaunaz

Sometimes we need a little encouragement to get back into the swing of things for school. When you or your children need to study, place a piece or two of charoite on the desk or table where homework is done. If necessary, these stones can be tucked into a desk drawer. Charoite has a distinctive color and patterns that aid in focusing the mind. Its energy also builds dedication to learning. Beryl is another stone that works well for this purpose.

DISSOLVE STRESS

After relaxing during the summer, the start of the school year and switching gears into autumn can add stress to our lives. Set aside time for a soak in the tub and have a piece of blue lace agate, labradorite, or sodalite handy. Hold the stone between your hands and visualize all your stress going into the stone. When you are finished with your bath, place the stone by the tub drain—make sure it will not go down—and let the water carry your stress away.

— • • • —

Blue sodalite is reminiscent of lapis lazuli
because it is sometimes a component of that stone.
Even though sodalite is sometimes used
as a substitute for lapis lazuli,
it does not have a glittery appearance
because it lacks pyrite inclusions.

OPEN UP FOR DREAMWORK

Effective dreamwork does not just happen; we need to prepare for it. Place a few drops of rosemary essential oil on a cotton ball, and then put it in a small, organza sachet with a piece of chalcedony or phenacite. Position the sachet on your bedside table or hang it from a bedpost. These stones stimulate psychic energy for dreaming and aid in interpreting their meanings. During the day, tuck the sachet away in a drawer or keep it with your magic or divination gear.

CELEBRATE HATHOR

One of Hathor's feast days was held around this time of year. To the ancient Egyptians, this goddess of love, the sky, and the sun was important to many aspects of life and death. Place several pieces of turquoise and/or hawk's-eye on your altar to honor her. Use one of these stones as an amulet to call on her power when needed. Turquoise is instrumental when seeking truth and wisdom and hawk's-eye is especially good for warding off negativity.

— • • • —

Inscriptions in a temple to Hathor on the Sinai Peninsula
referred to her as the Lady of the Turquoise Country.
Hawk's-eye is another appropriate crystal for this goddess
because of her connection with Horus, the hawk-headed sky god.

Coming to the aid of our friends is important, but it can present challenges. If you feel drained when helping friends deal with their emotions or difficult situations, carry or wear two pieces of tourmaline—one pink and one black—to aid you. These stones will filter and ground emotionally charged energy allowing you to provide support and keep your own energy balanced.

• • •

Tourmaline can be black, blue, brown,
colorless, green, pink, red, or yellow.
Most are usually multicolored and crystals often
have different colors at opposite ends.
Like amber and topaz, it can become electrically
charged attracting dust and other small particles.

BUILD PROSPERITY FOR CHARITY

When cash flow does not coincide with the amount of charitable giving you have in mind, try this: Place your checkbook on your altar with a piece of opal and a pearl on top of it. Hold your hands over them as you say three times:

Stone of opal, beautiful pearl,
stir up cash, money swirl.
May prosperity flow to me,
so I can give it to charity.

Leave the checkbook and stones in place for three days.

SEPTEMBER 20
STIR UP GOOD KARMA

Get your good karma flowing out to the world by wearing or carrying apache tears. In addition to building good energy, these stones bring the body, mind, and spirit into balance. Keep a few apache tear crystals on your desk at work to maintain a steady flow of positive energy around you. The grounding energy of this stone also protects anyone wearing it from negative energy.

• • •

Apache tear is the name given
to small rounded pebbles of obsidian.
According to legend, these crystals are found
where Native Americans died.
Apache tear is a popular stone used in
Native American jewelry and amulets.

Use a piece of jet to energize and strengthen a pledge. Hold the stone between your hands as you review in your mind the purpose and desired outcome of your pledge. Continue to hold the stone as you recite your pledge, and then end by saying:

> *On this stone, I swear it be*
> *with every breath within me.*

Jet is also instrumental in binding spells, which can help support the pledge you have made.

MABON, THE AUTUMN EQUINOX

On this day of balance between light and dark, Mabon is a celebration of the beauty and bounty of the earth. In addition to giving thanks for abundance and blessings, it is an opportune time to acknowledge the fruit of the metaphorical seeds we have symbolically sewn in our lives. Crystals that support the energy of this sabbat include agate, chrysoprase, garnet, rhodochrosite, and zircon. Place them on your altar for ritual or hold one while meditating on your blessings.

Libra brings a period of seeking balance and promoting fairness. This is also a time to focus on fostering peace in relationships. Cooperation and unity are hallmarks of Libra. This period is also an opportune time for spells involving love and romance. Crystals that are especially effective to use with this sign include ametrine, beryl, chrysoprase, desert rose, diamond, kunzite, kyanite, lapis lazuli, moonstone, opal, peridot, rose quartz, and smoky quartz. Emerald, lepidolite, malachite, and red zircon are also associated with Libra. In the past, agate and beryl were considered particularly lucky for people born under this sign.

FIND YOUR INNER BEAUTY

Acknowledging our inner beauty is not a narcissistic act, it is a stepping-stone for a healthy and deeper sense of self. Fill a wide, shallow bowl with water. Place a piece of blue apatite in the water, and then lean over to gaze at your reflection. After studying your face for a few minutes, remove the stone from the water. Hold it against your heart and let its energy fill you with appreciation and acceptance of who you are. This stone is especially helpful in finding love and harmony within.

• • •

The mineral name for this variety of apatite is moroxite. This stone ranges from blue to greenish blue and is often strongly dichroic, appearing blue or yellow from different angles.

MANAGE YOUR TIME

Time management takes work, but, of course, a crystal can help. If you feel that life is chaotic or that the details of your schedule are getting away from you, use lepidolite to help bring order. Whatever method you use for keeping tabs on your schedule—calendar, appointment book, or cell phone—place a piece of lepidolite with it at night. This stone will also aid in focusing your attention.

SEPTEMBER 26
CELEBRATE A GOLDEN AUTUMN

As a reminder to get outside and enjoy the season, place pieces of citrine, sunstone, and topaz along a windowsill in your house where you will see them often. Alternatively, place them anywhere sunlight will reach them and boost the warmth of their colors. Don't limit this to your home; keep a set of these stones at work to aid you in taking refreshing breaks.

• • •

Prized for jewelry since ancient times,
citrine was also known as sunstone
and believed capable of holding sunlight.
Ranging from pale to dark yellow to golden brown,
darker stones are sometimes called Madeira citrine.

SEPTEMBER 27
BANISH BAD MEMORIES

It happens to everyone; from time to time our minds get stuck in a loop replaying unpleasant memories. If this occurs, use chrysoprase to break and banish these thoughts. Hold the stone as you briefly replay the memories in your mind, and then visualize sending them into the chrysoprase. Burn a pinch of mugwort and pass the stone through the smoke as you visualize these memories being carried away and dissipated.

Gebo represents generosity and the gift of hospitality. This rune marks a period of balance and sharing. It is also a time for building harmony in your life. Use chrysocolla, garnet, or larimar in spells to help bring these qualities into your life. To foster generosity, wear or carry angelite, cat's-eye, or chrysoberyl as an amulet. Also, place these crystals on your altar and give thanks for the gifts you have been given.

Figure 27: The rune Gebo

SEPTEMBER 29
BLESS YOUR MEALS

Although we can zip out to the supermarket and get whatever we want whenever we want, expressing gratitude for our food can be a meaningful practice, especially in this time of harvesting and gathering in. Begin by consecrating pieces of moss agate and blue topaz. Crumble a big pinch of dried chamomile or lavender in your cauldron or other place where you can safely burn them. Pass the crystals through the smoke as you say:

> *By herb, smoke, and ember,*
> *help me to always remember*
> *the earth and cycles that create food,*
> *so I may show my gratitude.*

When you set the table for meals, include these stones as a reminder of the power and blessings of nature.

THE CELTIC OGHAM GORT, MONTH OF IVY BEGINS

The Ogham Gort teaches us about strength and endurance, death and immortality. It is a symbol of the knowledge of things that are hidden and mysterious. This Ogham provides a time to enter the darkness within to find the symbolic jewels. Meditate with a clear quartz crystal to find your hidden jewels. Because Gort is associated with ivy, which frequently grows in a spiral, use pieces of serpentine to create a spiral shape on your altar to symbolize your spiritual journey through the wheel of the year.

Figure 28: The Ogham Gort

CHAPTER 11

OCTOBER

This turning of the wheel of the year brings dramatic changes as summer becomes a fond memory and night brings a chill to the air. Trees blaze into brilliant colors matched only by the splendor of gemstones.

October Birthstones

American: opal, tourmaline (traditional)

British: opal, tourmaline (alternate)

Others: aquamarine, garnet, kunzite, morganite (a pink variety of beryl), sapphire

European fifteenth to twentieth century: beryl, opal

This Month's Full Moon

This full moon is known as the Blood Moon, Hunter's Moon, and Harvest Moon. It marks a time of healing and stability, inspiration and courage. As the earth prepares for sleep, we prepare for our journey through the dark of the year. This moon also supports memories in preparation for Samhain. Crystals that are especially effective for the energy of this esbat include aquamarine, garnet, kunzite, morganite beryl, opal, sapphire, and tourmaline.

OCTOBER 1
TAKE THE LEAD

Don't feel intimidated by or shy away from taking a leadership role, especially if you are capable and have the necessary skills. Carry or wear amazonite to support you when you assume such a position. This stone keeps energy grounded and aids in communication. Amazonite brings stability and helps build relationships based in trust. It will also help you to inspire others and build group unity.

• • •

Although this stone was named for the Amazon River,
it is not found in the immediate vicinity of the river.
In fact, it is found in several other locations around the world.
The ancient Egyptians used amazonite for talismans,
figurines of deities, and kohl makeup pots.

CALL ON YOUR GUARDIAN ANGEL

A feast to honor guardian angels was first observed on this date in the sixteenth century (Finley 1993, 22). Light a white candle and place a piece or two of angelite, blue lace agate, danburite, or pink beryl on your altar to honor your guardian angel. These stones are also effective for calling on angels to aid you in magic work. While all four of these stones provide support for working with angels, angelite and danburite are especially helpful to heighten awareness.

• • •

*Known for its perfect and often large crystals,
beryl can grow up to three feet long and sometimes longer.
Both carved and rough beryl crystals have been used
for divination. During the Middle Ages, a crystal ball
was often referred to as a beryl.*

OCTOBER 3
CALL IN A DEBT

When someone owes you money, it can cause friction in a relationship. Use a little magic to smooth the way and speed up the process of receiving the money back. Hold a piece of tiger's-eye, say the person's name three times, then say:

Tiger's-eye, tiger's-eye,
to this person message fly.
Draw this money back to me;
with good haste, so mote it be.

Afterward, place the stone with your checkbook or financial papers.

One downside to autumn is that its blazing colors last for such a short time. Hold on to the beauty and energy of autumn by placing groups of gemstones around your home. This will also serve as a reminder of the blessings of this season. Use orange calcite, citrine, topaz, and red or yellow zircon to draw on the energy of autumn. Leave the crystals in place until you decorate for Yule.

— • • • —

A former name for red zircon, hyacinth specifically referred to yellow red or reddish brown stones. That name and variations of it were also used for some varieties of beryl, garnet, quartz, and spinel. Red zircon has also been known as jachant and jacinth.

October 5
REGAIN CONFIDENCE

Sometimes an event in our lives can knock us for a loop and shake faith in our abilities. If this happens, don't let it get the better of you. Place a piece of larimar on your desk as you make a list of all your strengths and skills. Don't be shy or egotistical—let truth guide you. Each night before going to bed, hold the larimar as you read the list. Place them on your bedside table overnight where you will see them first thing in the morning.

OCTOBER 6
AVOID DANGER

Any time that you feel threatened, especially when traveling, wear or carry a piece of sard to help protect you against danger. Be mindful and pay attention to your inner voice. This stone usually works through intuition to keep you alert in situations and guide you away from negative forces. That said, don't be foolhardy; always take necessary precautions to avoid trouble.

OCTOBER 7
HONOR MA'AT

Around this time of year, the ancient Egyptians held a feast for Ma'at, the goddess of truth and justice. Honor her by placing jade and/or turquoise on your altar or by wearing a piece of jewelry with either of these stones. In addition, use jade for spellwork to call on her for support when you are seeking the resolution of a legal matter or justice in the courts.

• • •

According to Egyptian mythology,
Ma'at was involved in determining
whether or not a deceased person's soul
could proceed to the netherworld.
If they had been truthful,
their heart would balance the scales with a feather.
Jade is associated with truth and turquoise with balance.

WORK TOGETHER

Because life is not always the bowl of cherries we would like it to be, we are sometimes faced with challenging people with whom we need to get along. A positive attitude helps, even though it may be difficult to maintain at times. As we know, a little magic can go a long way to help us. Use spinel as a charm to foster cooperation and remove obstacles. Wear or keep it with you as needed. This crystal also aids in setting a purpose and attaining success.

• • •

Myanmar (formerly Burma) has been a major source of spinel since ancient times. According to folklore, perfect spinel crystals were cut and polished by spirits.

OCTOBER 9
CALL ON FELICITAS

The ancient Romans considered several days throughout the year as particularly lucky. On these days, they celebrated Felicitas. This goddess personified personal good fortune and happiness. To call on her power for spells to attract luck and prosperity, use cat's-eye, chrysoprase, or Herkimer diamond. To attract happiness, wear any of these stones or place them around your home. In addition, these crystals are especially effective where money or relationships are concerned.

OCTOBER 10
RESOLVE A CONFLICT

As we all know, relationships are often complicated and sometimes disagreements arise. When this happens within your household, gather as many small pieces of chrysocolla as you can. Place them in a bowl and hold your hands over it as you say:

Chrysocolla, cool and calm,
may your energy become a balm.
Bring this conflict to an end;
may all feelings heal and mend.

Place the stones around your home until the situation is resolved.

October 11

The Meditrinalia, Day of Healing

Derived from the word *mederi* meaning "to be healed," the *Meditrinalia* was a Roman custom where old and new wines were mixed and tasted as a form of ritual healing (Hornblower, et al. 2012, 924). To symbolically call on the energy of the Meditrinalia, place grape-sized pieces of amethyst in a wine glass and charge them with healing energy as you say:

Amethyst stones, color of wine,
store this healing energy of mine.
Until it is needed by someone ill,
stay strong and pure, this is my will.

Afterward, wrap the stones in a white cloth and store them until needed.

OCTOBER 12
BIND IT IN ICE

Use a binding spell to help stop bullying or other negative behavior that is directed toward you. After lighting a black candle, hold a piece of obsidian between your hands. Visualize sending the bad behavior and energy of the person causing the problem into the stone. Place the obsidian in a small paper cup and fill it with enough water to cover the stone. Store the cup in the back of your freezer until the situation improves.

• • •

The Romans used obsidian for jewelry,
decorative objects, and amulets.
During the Middles Ages,
flat slabs of highly polished obsidian
were used as scrying mirrors.
John Dee reputedly owned one.

Wunjo brings in a period of joy and happiness, success and prosperity. This is an opportune time to foster friendships and build community cooperation. On a personal level, Wunjo shows us that true joy comes from within and is not something than can be bought or given to us by others. To work with the energy of this rune for spells or meditation, use aventurine and iolite together.

Figure 29: The rune Wunjo

OCTOBER 14
CREATIVITY KICK START

Sometimes we need a little help to get into the right mind-set for a creative project. One way is to use a somewhat flat piece of white quartz or black agate. Hold the stone between your palms for a few minutes, and then prop it on end so the largest and flattest surface is toward you on your desk or other workspace. Visualize the stone as a blank canvas or empty blackboard emanating inspiration and coaxing your creativity to action.

• • •

The Romans were especially fond of agate for signet rings.
During the Middle Ages, it was highly valued
and often used as talismans for luck.
Black agate can be completely black
or it may have some white banding.

FOSTER BEAUTY AND COMFORT

While magazines may inspire us to create a spectacular home, it takes more than store-bought items to create just the right energy that suits us. Known as a stone of abundance, rhodochrosite is effective for enhancing the energy of our surroundings, making a house truly a home. Place several pieces of rhodochrosite around your home in strategic locations such as the front door, family room, and kitchen to foster this energy.

SOLAR-POWERED MAGIC

Power your spells and any magical endeavor with energy from the sun. Place pieces of yellow beryl, orange calcite, citrine, and/or sunstone on a windowsill where they will catch the daylight. It doesn't have to be bright and sunny outside to activate a stone's connection with the sun. After several hours, wrap the stones in a yellow cloth until you are ready to use them.

• • •

Sunstone can be orange, reddish brown, or pale yellow.
Occasionally the sparkly sheen has a blue or green tinge.
Flakes of hematite and/or goethite are responsible
for the stone's glittering reflections.

PSYCHIC PROTECTION BRACELET

Purchase enough blue calcite beads to make a bracelet. As you string them together chant:

> *With beads of blue, a bracelet I make*
> *to cast a circle that nothing can break.*
> *Keep me protected as this I wear,*
> *and psychic energy may it share.*

After placing the bracelet on your arm, turn around slowly to cast a magic circle. Continue to wear the bracelet as you go about your magic work or ritual.

OCTOBER 18
BALANCE YOUR ENERGY

If you are feeling a little energetically out of sorts, use two pieces of sodalite to bring you into balance. Begin by holding a stone in each hand. Keep one arm down at your side as you raise the other one straight overhead. Visualize the stones creating a sphere of energy around you that follows an invisible wheel held by the arc of your arms. As you do this, become aware of the soothing energy emanating from the sodalite and bringing you into balance.

• • •

In addition to sometimes having white veins of calcite,
blue sodalite can have a tinge of violet coloring.
This stone's name refers to its sodium content.

OCTOBER 19
DON'T GIVE UP HOPE

With life's ups and downs, it is important to stay focused and not give up on the things you hope for. After all, our hopes and dreams bring fullness to our lives and provide meaningful goals. Wear or take time to sit quietly as you hold a piece of amazonite. In addition to fostering hope, this stone brings strength and success. It works well as a charm to help you stay optimistic and bring your dreams to fruition.

OCTOBER 20
CALLING OPPORTUNITY

Don't just sit and wait for opportunity to come knocking at your door, send out the message that you are looking for it. Hold several pieces of aventurine and/or calcite as you think about the type of circumstances for which you are looking. While it is important to be realistic, don't be afraid to aim high. Place the stones on several tables or shelves around your house as you say:

Opportunity, come to me;
manifest what I see.

OCTOBER 21
CATCH A FALLING STAR

Usually occurring between October 17 and 26, the Orionid meteor showers can be seen in all parts of the sky. Stand in front of your altar and visualize drawing down the power of these meteorites into pieces of red agate and/or carnelian. Use these energized stones to add fiery power to your spells. Especially good for protective spells, red agate also bolsters determination and aids in overcoming obstacles. Also a protective stone, carnelian fosters success.

• • •

Abundant as pebbles in many riverbeds
in India and in the Egyptian desert,
carnelian was used throughout
the ancient world for amulets.
Carnelian was also believed to
protect the dead in the afterlife.

This sign brings a period of deep emotion that is often associated with sex, darkness, death, and power. Scorpio provides access and opportunity to deal with these and other aspects of ourselves that we usually keep private. In addition, this is a good time to work on psychic abilities and to foster creativity. Crystals that are especially effective when working with the energy of Scorpio include alexandrite, beryl, bloodstone, carnelian, citrine, red jasper, labradorite, malachite, obsidian, rutilated quartz, rhodochrosite, and ruby. Snakeskin agate, kunzite, moonstone, opal, topaz, and turquoise are also associated with it. In the past, amethyst was considered particularly lucky for people born under this sign.

October 23
Take Time for Healing

Being the color of warm Caribbean waters, larimar fosters healing and harmonious energy. Place a piece of larimar next to your pillow while you take a nap or on the side of your bathtub as you take a healing soak so you can draw in its gentle energy. Before falling asleep or as you sit in the tub, say:

Larimar, Caribbean blue,
help me rest and renew.
Like a warm, healing sea,
surround me with tranquility.

Visualize yourself sitting on a beach at the edge of the water with gentle waves lapping at your feet. Feel the warmth of the sand and ocean surrounding you with soothing energy. Larimar will hold this energy for you so you can access it any time.

OCTOBER 24
ATTRACT ROMANCE

Sometimes in order to attract love and romance we need to start by being receptive to it. To help, use pieces of rose quartz and/or pink or red tourmaline. Lay out the crystals in the shape of a heart on your altar. Hold your hands a few inches above the stones to absorb their loving energy. These crystals will also help to keep your emotions on an even keel.

• • •

Almost everything about rose quartz
hints at love starting with its name.
The rose has been one of the greatest symbols of love.
Rose quartz has been linked with a love goddess
through the nickname of Venus's eyelid.
And, of course, its color whispers "romance."

INCREASE AND PROTECT MONEY

When we set out to raise our financial prospects, we should also think about protecting them. Light two candles on your altar—one green and one black. Place two dollar bills between the candles with a piece of malachite on top of them. Visualize the dollars growing into a stack of money as you say three times:

Malachite, malachite, please bring more;
keep all my money safe and secure.

Leave this in place for three days, and then store the stone where you keep your checkbook or financial records.

Call for Clarity

Before engaging in psychic work or making any kind of important decision, it is helpful to clear your mind of distracting thoughts. Hold a piece of clear calcite or clear quartz in each hand for a couple of minutes, and then place them against your temples. Move your awareness to the crystals and visualize their energy moving through your brain, subduing the clutter of thoughts, and bringing clarity.

OCTOBER 27
FAREWELL FAIRIES

According to many legends, the fairies return to their hills (*sidhe*) at Samhain and remain there until Beltane. Bid them farewell for the season by placing pieces of amber, chiastolite andalusite, danburite, jade, clear quartz, or staurolite around your garden or porch. Alternatively, take the stones to an area where you have felt their presence or choose a quiet, out-of-the-way spot. Also, place a small bowl of milk with the stones as a farewell toast.

• • •

Chiastolite is an opaque variety of andalusite
that is popular for the pronounced X or cross pattern
that is revealed when a crystal is cut horizontally.
It was worn in medieval times as a charm
for good luck as well as an amulet for protection.

October 28

The Celtic Ogham Ngetal, Month of Reed Begins

Ngetal can be a period of unexpected changes and challenges that require adaptability. Like the reed, Ngetal represents adaptability and the ability to bend in a situation rather than break. The message of this Ogham is to bide your time because with determination you can reach your goals. The energy of this Ogham provides support for self-work, especially for healing. Use green jasper, opal, or spinel to call on the energy of Ngetal.

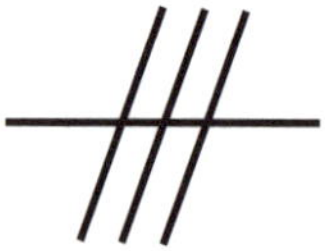

Figure 30: The Ogham Ngetal

The rune Hagalaz marks a period that is potentially chaotic and unsettling. Like the Celtic Ogham Ngetal, Hagalaz brings a time of change that requires the ability to adapt to changing situations. It is also a time of awakening through which we can find freedom and inner harmony. To work with the energy of this rune, use tiger's-eye or sodalite with selenite for spells, rituals, and meditation.

Figure 31: The rune Hagalaz

OCTOBER 29
CALL ON SPIRIT GUIDES

As the veil between the worlds grows thin, call on your spirit guides to aid you during this period of remembrance. Hold a piece of diopside and hiddenite to aid you when you speak to them. Hiddenite opens the channels to communicate with spirit guides and diopside keeps us grounded and balanced when working with other realms. Keep the stones on your altar until after Samhain.

• • •

Hiddenite is a variety of spodumene
discovered around the turn of the twentieth century.
Although its name may suggest an association with secrets,
it was named for William Hidden (1853–1918),
the geologist who discovered it.

PREPARE FOR YOUR ANCESTORS

This is a good day to prepare your home for ancestral spirits with an energy cleansing of the thresholds. Go to each exterior door and use a large piece of aquamarine to trace the outline of the doorframe as though you are cutting a big rectangle in the air in front of it. This crystal will purify the area around the door and banish any negative energy before it can enter your home.

OCTOBER 31
SAMHAIN

Samhain is a time to remember and honor loved ones, distant ancestors, and even pets who have passed. It is a night to invite their spirits to come close. Samhain is also a night for divination to call on the wisdom of ancestors. Gemstones that aid in working with the energy of this sabbat include carnelian, obsidian, onyx, spider web jasper, and white quartz. Also, consider including the birthstones of family members who have passed on your ritual altar.

CHAPTER 12

NOVEMBER

This month ushers in a time that is betwixt and between. As November brings us into the dark of the year, crystals light the way for the return of the sun at Yule. They also serve as guides to travel inward for self-exploration.

November Birthstones

American: citrine, topaz (traditional)
British: citrine (alternate), topaz
Others: beryl, chrysoberyl, yellow sapphire, tiger's-eye
European fifteenth to twentieth century: pearl, topaz

This Month's Full Moon

This full moon is known as the Beaver Moon, Mourning Moon, Snow Moon, and White Moon. November is a time for turning inward to discover the well of potential within, which will enable us to move forward and grow. This is also a time of cooperation and hope. The energy of this moon is conducive for divination and healing. Crystals that are especially effective for this esbat include beryl, cat's-eye, diopside, fluorite, hiddenite, jasper, jet, and topaz. Chrysoberyl, citrine, and yellow sapphire are also associated with this moon.

NOVEMBER 1 AND 2
DAY OF THE DEAD, ALL SAINTS' DAY, AND ALL SOULS' DAY

The days following Samhain continue to be important for honoring the dead. Like many sacred Pagan observances, this was adapted into the Christian calendar. The act of honoring loved ones and ancestors is observed around the world in various ways. Whether or not you hold a feast of the dead or set an extra place at dinner, make a circle with apache tears, jade, and/or jet on your table in remembrance.

— • • • —

The Romans used jet for jewelry and protective amulets.
In the nineteenth century, it was favored for jewelry
and made more popular by Queen Victoria when she wore it
while mourning the death of her beloved husband, Prince Albert.

NOVEMBER 3

POST-SAMHAIN ALTAR CLEANING

After sabbat rituals, it is important to clean our altars and freshen the space around them. After Samhain it is especially important as we leave our deceased loved ones behind and move forward to Yule and rebirth. After smudging with herbs or incense to purify your sacred space, place a piece of hematite, moldavite, or white quartz at each corner of your altar for a couple of days to bless and reconsecrate it.

— • • • —

Throughout the ancient world, hematite was crushed and used as a pigment called red ochre. It was used in burials to represent the transformation and rebirth of the deceased. Hematite was also used for ceremonial and talismanic purposes.

NOVEMBER 4
LUNAR HEALING

Regardless of the moon phase, Luna can be called upon for healing energy. Hold a piece of moonstone or selenite in each hand as you draw down lunar energy. Visualize this shimmering, calming energy surrounding you, uniting body, mind, and spirit and bringing you into wholeness. You can also send this healing energy to others. Afterward, wrap the stone in a white cloth and store it with your ritual or magical gear.

NOVEMBER 5
CONTROL YOURSELF

Whether we fall head over heels in love, get carried away playing a game, or impulsively engage in an activity, sometimes we may need to exercise self-control. Two stones that are particularly helpful are onyx and sardonyx. Onyx consists of alternating layers of black and white. Despite what its name suggests, sardonyx consists of alternating bands of reddish brown sard and white chalcedony. Prepare your stone by holding it between your hands and saying:

With two colors; one dark, one light,
help me find balance and do what is right.

Keep the stone with you or place it in your home where you will see it often. It will serve as a reminder that self-discipline is not a punishment but a means to deal with something that could be potentially harmful.

NOVEMBER 6
INCREASE MAGICAL POWER

Before engaging in ritual, divination, or any magical activity, it is important to prepare your energy. Hold a piece of amber between your palms for a moment or two, and then place it against your heart. Visualize the crystal's pulsing, golden energy spreading throughout your body and surrounding you in its powerful glow. In addition to boosting magical strength, amber provides stability and protection.

The dark of the year presents a quiet time for reflection and introspection. Often, along with turning inward comes deeper spiritual meaning and growth. Hold a piece of ametrine during meditation to help bring clarity to thoughts that arise during contemplation. Over time, this practice aids in reaching a higher level of awareness that can enhance magic work, divination, and other practices. This is also helpful for keeping energy grounded during the holiday season.

—— • • • ——

Just as its name suggests, this stone is a combination of amethyst and citrine. It has distinct bands of purple amethyst and brownish-yellow citrine. Although these colors are across from each other on the color wheel, this pairing of complementary opposites creates a balance of energies.

NOVEMBER 8
DRAW IN THE SUNSHINE

During this period of long nights and short days, many of us may struggle with the reduced amount of sunlight. This is known as Seasonal Affective Disorder (SAD). In addition to the everyday methods for dealing with it, use a little magic to help you. On sunny days, place pieces of amber, citrine, and/or sunstone on your windowsills. On overcast days, hold these stones and visualize the warmth and light of a sunny day.

NOVEMBER 9
CALL ON EARTH ENERGY

Whenever you need strength and balance for magic or everyday life, use moss agate. Stand with your arms relaxed at your sides as you hold one of these crystals in each hand. Slowly and mindfully, visualize drawing earth energy up through your body. Although your feet and legs may feel slightly heavy at first, your heart and mind will surge with energy and power. Moss agate also helps to balance the emotions and foster harmony.

DISPEL NEGATIVITY IN RELATIONSHIPS

If bad feelings have developed in a relationship, use a piece of larimar to aid you in reconciling the situation. Write the name of the person on a piece of tissue paper. Fold it small and hold it between your palms with the stone as you say three times:

Larimar, stone of blue,
help this relationship to be true.

Place the stone on your altar and the paper in a cup of water. When the paper disintegrates, pour the water outside on the ground.

This is a day to honor all those who have gone to war. Lay out pieces of brown agate on your altar in the shape of a circle or heart. Hold your hands above the stones as you visualize sending healing energy to veterans. If you know a vet personally, place his or her picture on your altar along with the stones. If you are attending a parade or other event, carry one of the stones in your pocket.

Also called a *way stone*, lodestone is a guide and guardian. Wear this crystal in jewelry or carry a piece of lodestone when you go for a walk. Don't have a route in mind? Let the stone guide you. Stay alert and pay close attention to where you go and what you see as you may be presented with important signs. Take note of anything unusual as its meaning may be revealed later. Lodestone is also an aid for finding the appropriate spiritual path.

• • •

While the Chinese used lodestone
for a simple type of compass around 100 BCE,
the first mention of such an invention in Europe did not
occur until 1190 (Merrill, et al., 1998, 3).

The rune Nauthiz presents us with the opportunity to see that what we may believe to be limitations inflicted upon us may actually be self-imposed obstacles. Nauthiz helps us review and perceive these situations with clarity. It also helps us muster the power to make the necessary changes in our lives to overcome these obstacles. Spend time in meditation with hematite and peridot or sugilite to work with the energy of this rune.

Figure 32: The rune Nauthiz

Psychic work, divination, and dreamwork require clarity of vision, allowing us to "see" with an inner eye. Apophyllite, clear calcite, and clear quartz are especially helpful in opening the gates of the mind to look inward and to create a channel through which information can be received. Prepare your crystal by attuning it to your energy. Hold it between your hands in front of your heart and simply pay attention to any sensations you may feel from the crystal. When you sense a shift in energy, hold the crystal in front of your third eye chakra until you feel another shift in energy. This means that the stone is ready. Wrap it in a white cloth and put it away until you need it. Before using the crystal in a session, hold it between your palms for a moment to stimulate energy and open psychic channels.

Before working with animals at a shelter or with your own pets, sit quietly for about five minutes while you hold a piece of hawk's-eye against your heart. Afterward, place it in your pocket. This stone helps to calm and balance energy and heightens awareness to receive vibrations from animals. Hawk's-eye is also instrumental when calling on animals to aid in magic work and healing.

NOVEMBER 16
THE NIGHT OF HECATE

Hecate is a threefold goddess and great crone. She presides over crossroads and helps us see where we have been, where we currently are—and most importantly—where we can go. She does not predict the future, but she reveals our potentials and the possible paths that may be open to us. Place a piece of moonstone on your altar and light a black candle to honor her and call on her wisdom for insight.

— • • • —

Hecate strongly echoes the very ancient Great Mother Goddess. She presided over birth and life but more importantly death with the hope of regeneration. Hecate was also regarded as having power over the hidden forces of nature.

NOVEMBER 17
THE LEONID METEOR SHOWERS

Active through most of the month, these meteor showers peak around this time and appear in all parts of the sky. Although the point from which they radiate is an illusion, they seem to come from the constellation Leo the Lion. After drawing down the energy of these meteorites with bloodstone, hematite, or red zircon, use these stones to call on the power of the celestial lion to add strength to your magic work.

• • •

Bloodstone is also known as heliotrope.
This name comes from the Greek helios
and tropos, *meaning "sun turner,"*
which stems from the belief that it could
turn the sun's rays red (Schumann 2006, 144).

If you feel yourself getting angry with someone, roll a piece of howlite or peridot between your fingers as you say:

May this feeling growing in me
begin to fade and no longer be.
Destructive feelings cause nothing but pain;
no one wins, there's nothing to gain.

Hold the stone against your stomach and continue repeating this like a mantra until you feel calm.

FOSTER COOPERATION

A workplace where people are not focused on common goals creates fractured energy and problems for a business. To help remedy the situation, place several plants in key locations around the office where people frequently congregate. Place four pieces of fluorite or hematite in the cardinal directions in each flowerpot. These stones will strengthen connections, foster cooperation, and help everyone work toward a common goal.

• • •

The term fluorescence *was derived from the mineral fluorite because it was the first substance in which this light phenomenon—emitting light under ultraviolet light— was observed. Most types of fluorite exhibit a strong light blue or violet fluorescence.*

Coming most often from volcanoes and occasionally meteorites, peridot is a fiery gemstone that stimulates the development of psychic abilities, especially clairvoyance. Sit in front of your altar and sprinkle pieces of peridot in a starburst pattern outward from where you are sitting. Visualize the stones expanding your energy outward, helping you to connect with psychic vibrations.

With so much brutality in the news every day, we may sometimes steel our emotions to avoid becoming overwhelmed. Numbing our feelings makes us immune to some of the pain but it can also cut us off from other people. Keep a piece of green jasper in a heart-shaped box to help you deal with this situation. As an alternative, place the green jasper in a small box with a picture of a heart. When you feel alarmed or shocked about an event, open the box and gaze at the stone. Let it remind you that the strength of compassion and love can overcome adversity.

— • • • —

Ranging from pale to dark green,
this jasper represents the color of the heart chakra.
The ancient Egyptians carved green jasper
for amulets and funerary heart scarabs.

This is a period for thinking about the bigger things in life and to be unafraid to follow the beat of your own drum. Sagittarius helps us work on matters concerning the self, sexuality, and spirituality. This is a good time to follow intuition, engage in dreamwork, and to engage in travel that broadens our horizons. Crystals that are especially effective with this sun sign include amethyst, azurite, Herkimer diamond, iolite, yellow jasper, labradorite, obsidian, opal, sodalite, sphene, sugilite, topaz, turquoise, and black, green, or red tourmaline. Emerald, lapis lazuli, and ruby are also associated with Sagittarius. In the past, beryl and pearl were considered particularly lucky for people born under this sign.

NOVEMBER 23
MOVING INWARD
TO MOVE OUTWARD

The dark time of the year is conducive for turning inward and spending quiet time alone to reflect on life. Light one candle on your altar and hold a piece of tree agate. This stone invites us to look inward where we can find a quiet pool of energy. Tree agate is also instrumental for growth and will guide us outward to bloom and come into our personal power in the spring.

NOVEMBER 24
GAIN SHAMANIC INSIGHT

In addition to reflection and meditation, long nights are conducive for shamanic journeys and magic work. Keep a piece of leopard skin jasper in your pocket to connect with animal energy and magic as you traverse the realms. This stone will also keep you grounded to facilitate your return to this world with the wisdom you have gained. Also keep it nearby during divination sessions for extra insight into messages.

• • •

This variety of jasper is brown, grey,
or sandy colored with tan or black spots.
It was so named because the pattern
often resembles the skin of a leopard.
In addition, animals served as guides and guardians
to help shamans navigate between the worlds.

November 25

The Celtic Ogham Ruis, Month of Elder Begins

The Ogham Ruis is associated with the elder. Although this tree is not in bloom or fruiting at this time of year, the elder is a tree of the Crone. As we head into the darkest part of the year, Ruis bids us to see beyond the surface of things. It brings awareness to the cycles that punctuate our lives and provides energy conducive for divination. Use malachite or moldavite to draw on the power of this Ogham and the wisdom of the crone.

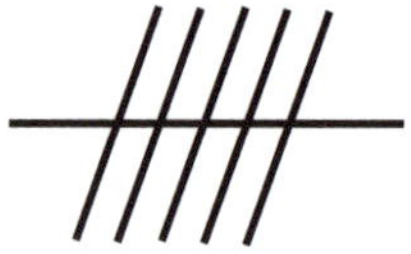

Figure 33: The Ogham Ruis

Whenever you feel the need to strengthen your connection with others, think of building a rainbow bridge to carry and manifest your thoughts. Sit in front of your altar and hold a piece of rainbow obsidian so its colorful sheen catches the light of a candle. After observing the dance of color, place the stone on your altar. Visualize an arch of rainbow colors emanating outward to those with whom you want to build community.

— • • • —

Although a rainbow bridge has been used as a metaphor for a path between earth and heaven when a pet passes on, the arching colors of the rainbow have long been a symbol of hope and connection.

NOVEMBER 27
BECOME LUCKY IN LOVE

All relationships take work, but a little bit of luck and crystal magic can be useful when it comes to love and marriage. Wear sardonyx jewelry to help draw that special someone to you. Alternatively, hold a piece of sardonyx as you send out your intentions in a spell. This stone also fosters good communication and peace, which are helpful in any relationship.

— • • • —

Like sard, sardonyx is also known as sard stone.
For centuries, both stones have been two
of the most widely used crystals for engraved jewelry.
Having two colors, sardonyx represents unity.

November 28
The Runic Half Month of Isa Begins

Associated with ice, the Isa rune ushers in a time for stillness; however, it does not mean that we become frozen. While this period may present challenges, it also provides an opportunity for clarity. In addition, this rune helps us tune into the depth and beauty of approaching winter. Because they resemble icicles, long clear quartz or clear calcite crystals are ideal for working with the energy of Isa.

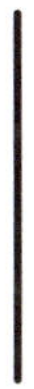

Figure 34: The rune Isa

Gearing up for the holidays is fun but it can also put a strain on schedules and sometimes relationships as we get together with extended family. To keep the energy of those negative nellies and drama queen relatives in check, place pieces of black tourmaline around your home where guests congregate. This stone will absorb and ground negativity while fostering cheerfulness.

─── • • • ───

*This opaque variety is the most
abundant type of tourmaline.
Its mineral name is schorl.
Thin, needlelike crystals
of schorl form tourmalated quartz.*

NOVEMBER 30
LET IT SNOW

If you enjoy outdoor activities in winter or just enjoy the beauty of a snowfall, sit in front of your altar with a piece of snowflake obsidian and a snow globe. Hold the stone in one hand and shake the snow globe with the other as you say:

Stone speckled with white,
on field dark as night.
Snow globe glow, let it snow.
Let it snow, let it snow.

NOTES

_____

_____

_____

_____

_____

_____

_____

_____

_____

_____

_____

_____

_____

_____

_____

_____

_____

_____

_____

_____

CHAPTER 13 ────────

DECEMBER

In this month of merry-making, we enjoy gathering bright things around us whether they shine from their own accord or reflect dancing candle-light. Sparkling gemstones enhance the season and our magic with their beauty and energy.

December Birthstones

American: blue topaz (traditional), tanzanite (a variety
of blue zoisite), turquoise (traditional), zircon
British: turquoise, zircon (alternate)
Others: aquamarine, blue topaz, chrysoprase
European fifteenth to twentieth century: bloodstone, ruby

This Month's Full Moon

The full moon of December is known as the Oak Moon (if
it falls before the winter solstice), Cold Moon, and Snow
Moon. As the year draws to a close, it is important to take
time to experience the peace, solace, and joy of this season.
Giving and sharing are meaningful hallmarks when done
from the heart. This is a good time to express devotion.
Crystals that are especially effective for this esbat include
angelite, aquamarine, bloodstone, chrysoberyl, ruby, smithsonite, and zircon. Blue topaz and turquoise are also associated with this moon.

With so many family members visiting this time of year, the energy of our homes may need some help. Collect pieces of apatite, celestine, and/or moss agate. Use these to lay out small spirals in the rooms where your family gathers, such as the kitchen, living room, or family room. Create the spirals on windowsills, tables, or even on the floor under a piece of furniture. Not only will they add to seasonal decorations, they will also help to keep a flow of calm energy through your home.

• • •

The spiral is one of the most common motifs in many cultures around the world and throughout time. The energy of the spiral is dynamic, yet grounding and centering. It moves inward and outward; gathering together and sending forth.

DECEMBER 2
SPREAD GOOD CHEER

Use this day to radiate heartfelt feelings and cheerfulness. Wear or carry a piece of apophyllite or turquoise to bolster your energy and send out good vibrations. Also, place a few of these crystals on windowsills around your home, in the glove box of your car, and on your desk at work to surround yourself and others with positive energy. Before going to bed, hold a piece of apophyllite or turquoise for a moment or two to invite sweet dreams.

— • • • —

Apophyllite and turquoise are associated with the zodiac constellation of Taurus, which is visible at night (in the Northern Hemisphere) lending its strength for magical purposes. Also associated with the element earth, both stones aid in staying grounded during this busy season.

DECEMBER 3
SPENDING SPELL

While we know that the true spirit of the season is not material, we may sometimes spend more money than we should. To keep your spending in check, before going shopping hold a piece of green tourmaline between your hands and say three times:

Stone of green, smooth and clean,
help me keep within my means.

Carry the stone in your purse or pocket when you head to the stores or place it next to your computer when shopping online.

DECEMBER 4
ALIGN WITH YOUR HEART

Occasionally, we are all faced with a situation where we feel that our hearts just aren't into something we have committed to doing. Trying to act with enthusiasm usually doesn't work, but aligning our feelings and thoughts can put us on the right track where we can gain a fresh perspective or decide on the right course of action. Take some time alone to sit quietly and hold a piece of smithsonite. When you begin to experience the calming effect of this stone, hold it against your heart for a moment, then against your forehead. When you touch it to your forehead say:

> *Balance my head and my heart,*
> *help me find the way to start.*

Allow the stone to work with your intuition and lead you to a solution that is right for you.

DECEMBER 5

PROTECTION FROM STORMS

To generate protective energy for your house, place pieces of jet in the cardinal directions inside on windowsills or outside of your home on the ground. After putting them in place, sit in front of your altar and visualize the energy of the stones, creating a protective dome over and around your home. Also, imagine a winter storm blowing around and above the house as you and your family stay safe and snug inside.

December 6
Peace on Earth

Gather enough pieces of aquamarine and/or larimar to create a circle on your altar—the stones don't need to touch each other. Hold your hands above the stones as you say:

> *May there be peace on earth;*
> *love, joy, and mirth.*
> *May there be no more fear;*
> *as we soon begin a new year.*

As you do this, visualize sending out energy with feelings of love and joy.

Although this is a time of year for drinking a toast to someone's health, we can also send our wishes with magic. Line up pieces of aventurine, jade, and/or jasper on a windowsill or shelf. Use one piece for each person to whom you want to wish health and prosperity for in the coming year. As you put each one in place, visualize sending your good thoughts their way.

———— • • • ————

While jade was used for protection against kidney disease during the Middle Ages, in the Chinese practice of feng shui, this stone is associated with general good health and long life.

December 8
Sort Yourself Out

The rush and excitement of the holidays can leave anyone feeling out of sorts. To bring your energy back into balance, use two pieces of staurolite. Hold one on top of your head and the other at your heart as you visualize moving your energy downward and away from you. Next, place the stones on the floor and cover them with your bare toes as you draw earth energy up through your body bringing balance and stability.

HONOR MOON GODDESSES

This date marks the first appearance of Our Lady of Guadalupe, the patron saint of Mexico, in 1531 at the former sacred hill of an Aztec moon goddess (Leeming and Page 1994, 163). Light a white candle on your altar and make a circle around the base of it with moonstone, pearls, and/or white quartz to honor your moon goddess of choice. If you have enough of these stones, add crescent moon shapes on both sides of the circle.

• • •

Moon goddesses include Aine, Aphrodite, Ariadne, Arianrhod, Artemis, Cerridwen, Chang Ngo, Diana, Freya, Hecate, Ishtar, Isis, Juno, Luna, Nanna, Persephone, Rhiannon, Sedna, and Selene.

DECEMBER 10
WITH VISIONS OF SUGAR PLUMS

To foster pleasant dreams and enhance dreamwork, place pieces of barite and chalcedony in a small organza bag to hang above your bed or on a bedpost. Add a piece of your favorite candy to the bag to symbolically sweeten your dreams. Both barite and chalcedony are an aid for remembering and interpreting dreams. In addition, barite supports astral work and chalcedony brings peaceful balance to the emotions.

— • • • —

When barite was discovered to be luminescent—
glowing in the dark for a time after being in bright light—
it was thought to be the long sought-after philosopher's stone.

DECEMBER 11

MELT YOUR PROBLEMS

Place a piece of sodalite in a small paper cup and pour in enough water to cover the stone. Hold the cup between your hands and visualize your problems going into the water. Put the cup in the freezer until the water turns to ice. When you take it out, peel the paper cup away and place the ice with the stone in a bowl. Now visualize your problems dissipating as the ice melts. Leave it in place overnight, and then toss the water and stone on the ground outside to finish the spell.

DECEMBER 12
COURAGE TO LIVE YOUR DREAM

Following a dream is not always easy. It takes courage to make the necessary changes to make it possible. Write down several keywords about the changes you want to manifest into reality that will allow you to follow your dream. Fold the paper and hold it between your hands with a piece of andalusite, a stone of manifestation. Close your eyes and think about the steps you will need to take, and then say:

Andalusite, please help me
achieve the dream that I can see.
With determination, I believe,
all these changes, I will achieve.

Keep the paper and stone on your desk or in a place where you will see it often and be reminded of what you need to do to reach your goal.

Jera brings us into a period of recognizing cycles, not just seasonal ones but the recurring events in our lives. This is a time to look back at what we have accomplished and to enjoy the reward our work has brought. Although the cycles of life constantly change, Jera reminds us to pause and appreciate success, prosperity, and peace when it occurs. Use moonstone and blue topaz to work with the energy of this rune.

Figure 35: The rune Jera

Visible in the Northern and Southern Hemispheres, the Geminids are a series of major meteor showers that peak around this time of the month. Scatter a handful of fiery stones such as fire agate, yellow beryl, orange calcite, red jasper, and/or red tourmaline on your altar to represent a meteor shower. Draw down the energy of the Geminids into the crystals by raising your hands to shoulder height, palms upward. Visualize pulling energy from the meteors down through your body. Let it build until you feel you cannot hold the energy any longer, and then place your hands above the crystals and release the energy into them. Allow the crystals to remain in place overnight, and then put them away until you need them to add power to a spell. Associated with the Gemini constellation, the energy of these meteor showers is doubled.

In this season of material madness, take some time to count your true blessings. For each good thing or person in your life that you want to acknowledge, place a piece of rose quartz in a decorative bowl. When you are finished, hold the bowl between your hands for a few minutes as you meditate on beauty and grace. Afterward, place the bowl among your Yule decorations to serve as a reminder throughout the season.

FOSTER FAITH

Wear a piece of diamond, iolite, or pearl jewelry to support and foster your faith. Before putting it on, hold the jewelry between your palms, close your eyes, and visualize your faith burning like an eternal flame in your soul. Wear the jewelry throughout the holiday season, and then place it on your altar on New Year's Eve to welcome a new year of beauty and faith.

— • • • —

Medieval stonecutters sought to increase the diamond's optical effects to bring out its brilliance and fire. It wasn't until the early twentieth century that the brilliant cut, also known as the diamond cut, was brought to a high level of perfection.

Create your own celebration for this lusty Roman festival by heightening the passion in your life. Wear a piece of jewelry with flame spinel, red spinel, or thulite zoisite on this day. Also, place these stones around your bedroom to enhance your lusty pleasure. Flame and red spinel are especially effective for sparking passion and romance. Thulite, a pink or red variety of zoisite, helps to kindle or rekindle passion in a sexual relationship.

December 18
Honor Epona

As the only Gaulish goddess officially honored in Rome, Epona was held in high esteem by the cavalry. Place a picture of a white horse on your altar and surround it with pieces of azurite to honor Epona. Also, call on her to aid you in working with animals and in further developing your magical skills. Azurite is a stone of awareness that helps to sharpen intuition and provide insight for divination and dreamwork.

DECEMBER 19
FIND A GIFT WITHIN

Sometimes the greatest gift we can receive comes from recognizing the talents we have to offer others. Hold a piece of bloodstone or charoite as you meditate on who you are and how your skills—even those that are only just developing—are of benefit to those around you. Do this without being egotistical and you will find a true gift.

— • • • —

According to mineralogist Mikhail Evdokimov,
the name charoite comes from the Russian word chary
because of the impression this stone gives—
chary *means "magic charm" (Evdokimov 1997, 74).*

This is a good time of year to work with angelic magic. Use angelite, blue lace agate, and/or morganite beryl on your altar to connect with angelic energy. Also, use these stones to call on their powers for the good of others. In addition, angelite is especially helpful to foster compassion and generosity, blue lace agate supports spiritual development, and morganite is an aid when seeking wisdom and guidance.

━━━ • • • ━━━

Whether you work with angels, magical beings,
or different spirits, the time around the winter solstice
is especially powerful. These three crystals can help you
tune into the magic in a meaningful way.

DECEMBER 21/22
YULE, THE WINTER SOLSTICE

The winter solstice is an event that has been celebrated by civilizations throughout time and around the world. As a time of transformation, Yule celebrates the return of the sun, which brings hope and the promise of ongoing life. Lay out pieces of amber, citrine, sunstone, and/or yellow jasper in a circle or sunburst pattern on your sabbat altar to connect with the power and transformative energy of Yule. Leave them in place until New Year's Eve.

Conducive to working with the material side of life, this is a time to concentrate on advancing oneself, setting goals, and achieving success. Magic focused on career can bring positive changes in preparation for the year ahead. Crystals that are particularly effective to work with the energy of Capricorn include agate, beryl, carnelian, cat's-eye, fluorite, hematite, jet, obsidian, smoky quartz, star sapphire, tiger's-eye, green tourmaline, and yellow zircon. Agate, amethyst, rose quartz, and ruby are also associated with Capricorn. In the past, onyx and ruby were considered especially lucky for people born under this sign.

DECEMBER 23
REMOVE TO RENEW

Gather several pieces of peridot and/or moldavite, and then go to a wooded area or pond. Think of all the things you want to purge from your life in preparation for the New Year. For each thing you want to release, toss a stone in the water or on the ground. When you finish, stand in silence for a moment or two, and then say:

With each thing that I release,
bring a feeling of true peace.
As I prepare for the New Year,
may it be filled with love and good cheer.

THE CELTIC OGHAM BEITH, MONTH OF BIRCH BEGINS

Beginning just after the winter solstice, the time of Beith continues through most of January. This Ogham carries us through the turning of the year and prepares the way for renewal. Carnelian epitomizes this period because its reddish color is associated with the rebirth of the sun. Use this stone and Ogham to mark renewal and initiate beginnings. Carnelian also aids in meeting challenges that may occur at this time of year.

Figure 36: The Ogham Beith

INVITE GRACE

Although this season is busy and we often feel rushed, when we take a little time for ourselves we can discover a peaceful state of grace within. The word *grace* can mean beauty and charm, but it also relates to a deep sense of harmony and flow of energy. Grace comes with feelings of gratitude, love, and awe. It can also be a sense of spiritual freedom and the feeling of having your place within the universe. It is a feeling of alignment with the goodness in the world. To help cultivate a feeling of grace, get up early in the morning and sit in front of your altar as you hold a piece of rose quartz in one hand and a piece of pink jasper in the other. Take a few minutes to simply enjoy this quiet time of day, and then review the things that you regard as blessings. Also think of things that you can do to bring blessings to others. Visualize a soft pink light emanating from the crystals, moving up your arms to your heart, and then out to the world.

DECEMBER 26
MAINTAIN ENERGY

The holidays can take a toll on our energy as we enjoy more social time and travel. In addition to looking after your health, spend a few moments each day holding a piece of kyanite or selenite. Not only do these stones boost energy, they also help to maintain clarity and keep stress at bay. In addition, kyanite provides focus to enhance and expand creative skills. Selenite draws on the cyclic power of renewal providing energy for new beginnings.

Known as Frau Holle to the Teutonic people of Northern Europe, her name comes from the Old Norse *hylja*, which means "to conceal" (McKinnell 2014, 42). According to some legends, Frau Holle produced snow that hid the landscape by shaking loose feathers from her pillows and comforter. Celebrate the wisdom of this crone and the beauty of winter by placing pieces of snowflake obsidian and white quartz on a windowsill. Add a pearl to further enhance the energy.

——— • • • ———

For thousands of years, pearls have been regarded
as one of the most valuable gems,
even serving as bling during the Stone Age.
While the most prized pearls come from oysters
in the genus Pinctada, *giant clams, giant conchs,*
and freshwater clams and mussels also produce them.

The Eiwaz rune ushers in a period of strength and trust. In community, we may be called upon to serve as a guardian and defend others. Magically, this rune can be called upon for protection as we fulfill this role and help others. On a personal level, this half month is a time to acknowledge and accept responsibility for how we conduct our lives. Angelite and blue lace agate are especially effective to draw on the power of Eiwaz.

Figure 37: The rune Eiwaz

DECEMBER 29
MAKE AN EASY TRANSITION

Even when we plan and prepare for changes in our lives, making the transition can sometimes be a bumpy road. Place pieces of chrysocolla or hessonite garnet around your home where you will see them often. Take a minute or two each day to hold one of the stones, which will keep your energy grounded. Chrysocolla is a stone of peace that aids in resolving problems, especially those that arise in a relationship. Hessonite provides emotional support and fosters courage to make important life changes.

• • •

Also known as cinnamon stone, hessonite ranges from orange to brownish orange and transparent to translucent. The Greeks and Romans used this stone for cameos and intaglio work. When placed in a gold setting, hessonite was believed to be a powerful talisman.

December 30

PLANT YOUR WISHES

Use a piece of moss agate or tree agate for each wish that you want to make for the coming year and plant them in a flowerpot with soil. Close your eyes and visualize a plant growing and each leaf that unfurls bringing one of your wishes true. Place the flowerpot on or beside your altar on New Year's Eve. Moss agate is a stone of abundance and hope and tree agate supports introspection, growth, and personal well-being.

DECEMBER 31
NEW YEAR'S EVE

We have come full circle through twelve months. As the wheel of the year makes its final turn and begins a new cycle, hold a piece of clear quartz and dioptase as you pause to reflect. Think about the path that brought you here and where it may lead you in the year to come, and then say:

As I look to the new year,
wondering what lies in store,
come what may, I have no fear,
my spirit is ready to help me soar.

Dioptase is a stone of abundance that fosters comfort, prosperity, and well-being. Clear quartz is a powerhouse that boosts the energy of other crystals.

NOTES

_____

_____

_____

_____

_____

_____

_____

_____

_____

_____

_____

_____

_____

_____

_____

_____

_____

_____

_____

_____

_____

Summary

As we have seen, the use of crystals and gemstones dates to very ancient times when they served as bling and so much more. While some gemstones attract our attention with rich colors, others seem to play with the light or shine from within. Regardless of their beauty, we are also attracted to certain crystals because of their energy. Crystals strengthen our connection with the natural world because they are formed by dynamic processes—the powerful creative and destructive forces of the earth.

Crystals provide a simple and effective way to add power to magic and ritual. In addition, the nuances of each stone's individual characteristics and energy can enrich our daily lives. Spend a little time getting to know your crystals for a rewarding and personal experience as you explore the magic that surrounds you.

Bibliography

Adkins, Lesley, and Roy A. Adkins. *Handbook to Life in Ancient Rome*. New York: Facts on File, 2004.

Altman, Jenifer. *Gem and Stone: Jewels of Earth, Sea, and Sky*. San Francisco: Chronicle Books, 2012.

Anonymous. *The Orphic Hymns*. Translated by Apostolos N. Athanassakis and Benjamin M. Wolkow. Baltimore: Johns Hopkins University Press, 2013.

Baur, Jaroslav, and Vladimir Bouška. *A Guide in Color to Precious & Semiprecious Stones*. Secaucus, NJ: Chartwell Books, 1989.

Bonnefoy, Yves, comp. *Roman and European Mythologies*. Translated by Wendy Doniger. Chicago: University of Chicago Press, 1992.

Bunson, Margaret R. *Encyclopedia of Ancient Egypt,* rev. ed. New York: Facts on File, 2002.

Chang, L. L. Y., R. A. Howie, and J. Zussman. *Rock-forming Minerals: Non-Silicates,* vol. 5B. Bath, England: Geological Society Publishing House, 1998.

Clucas, Stephen, ed. *John Dee: Interdisciplinary Studies in English Renaissance Thought.* Dordrecht, The Netherlands: Springer, 2006.

Collings, Michael R. *Gemlore: An Introduction to Precious and Semi-Precious Stones,* 2nd ed. Rockville, MD: Borgo Press, 2009.

Cryer, Max. *Superstitions and Why We Have Them.* Auckland, New Zealand: Exisle Publishing Limited, 2016.

Cunningham, Scott. *Cunningham's Encyclopedia of Crystal, Gem & Metal Magic.* St. Paul, MN: Llewellyn Publications, 2001.

Evdokimov, Mikhail D. "Charoite: A Unique Mineral from a Unique Occurrence" *Gems and Gemology,* vol. 33, no. 1, Spring 1997, 74.

Finlay, Victoria. *Jewels: A Secret History.* New York: Random House, 2007.

Finley, Mitch. *Everybody Has a Guardian Angel: And Other Lasting Lessons I Learned in Catholic Schools.* Eugene, OR: Wipf and Stock Publishers, 1993.

Hekster, Olivier, Sebastien Schmidt-Hofner, and Christian Witschel, eds. *Ritual Dynamics and Religious Change in the*

Roman Empire. Leiden, The Netherlands: Koninklijke Brill, NV, 2009.

Hornblower, Simon, Antony Spawforth, and Esther Eidinow, eds. *The Oxford Classical Dictionary*, 4th ed. Oxford, England: Oxford University Press, 2012.

Koehler, Cheryl Angelina. *Touring the Sierra Nevada*. Reno, NV: University of Nevada Press, 2007.

Kunz, George Frederick. *The Curious Lore of Precious Stones*. New York: J. B. Lippincott Company, 1913.

Leeming, David, and Jake Page. *Goddess: Myths of the Female Divine*. New York: Oxford University Press, 1994.

Lindsey, David Michael. *The Woman and the Dragon: Apparitions of Mary*. Gretna, LA: Pelican Publishing Company, 2000.

Mac Coitir, Niall. *Irish Trees: Myths, Legends, and Folklore*. Wilton, Ireland: Collins Press, 2006.

Manutchehr-Danai, Mohsen. *Dictionary of Gems and Gemology*. New York: Springer-Verlag, 2000.

Martimort, A. G., I. H. Dalmais, and P. Jounel, eds. *The Liturgy and Time: The Church at Prayer, An Introduction to the Liturgy*, vol. 4. Collegeville, MN: Liturgical Press, 1986.

McKinnell, John. *Essays on Eddic Poetry*. Donata Kick and John D. Shafer, eds. Toronto, Canada: University of Toronto Press, 2014.

Merrill, Ronald T., Michael W. McElhinny, and Phillip L. McFadden. *The Magnetic Field of the Earth: Paleomagnetism, the Core, and the Deep Mantle.* San Diego, CA: Academic Press, 1998.

Morris, Desmond. *Body Guards: Protective Amulets & Charms.* Shaftesbury, England: Element Books, 1999.

Oldershaw, Cally. *Firefly Guide to Gems.* Toronto, Canada: Firefly Books, 2003.

Payack, Paul J. J. *A Million Words and Counting: How Global English Is Rewriting the World.* New York: Citadel Press, 2008.

Pennick, Nigel. *The Pagan Book of Days: A Guide to Festivals, Traditions and Sacred Days of the Year.* Rochester, VT: Destiny Books, 2001.

Rapp, George R. *Archaeomineralogy.* New York: Springer-Verlag, 2002.

Ridpath, Ian. *Star Tales.* Cambridge, England: Lutterworth Press, 1988.

Roy, Christian. *Traditional Festivals: A Multicultural Encyclopedia,* vol. 2. Santa Barbara, CA: ABC-CLIO, 2005.

Sacks, David. *Encyclopedia of the Ancient Greek World.* New York: Facts on File, 2005.

Salzman, Michele Renee. *On Roman Time: The Codex—Calendar of 354 and the Rhythms of Urban Life in Late Antiquity.* Berkeley, CA: University of California Press, 1990.

Schumann, Walter. *Gemstones of the World,* 5th ed. New York: Sterling Publishing, 2006.

Shipley, Joseph T. *Dictionary of Word Origins.* New York: Dorset House, 1993.

Skeat, Walter W. *The Concise Dictionary of English Etymology.* Ware, England: Wordsworth Editions, 1993.

Sorrell, Charles A. *Rocks and Minerals: A Guide to Field Identification.* New York: St. Martin's Press, 2001.

Thompson, Jennifer Trainer. *The Joy of Family Traditions: A Season-by-Season Companion to Celebrations, Holidays, and Special Occasions.* Berkeley, CA: Celestial Arts, 2008.

Willis, Tony. *The Runic Workbook: Understanding and Using the Power of Runes.* New York: Sterling Publishing, 1986.

Wilson, Nigel, ed. *Encyclopedia of Ancient Greece.* New York: Routledge, 2006.

INDEX

To Write to the Author

If you wish to contact the author or would like more information about this book, please write to the author in care of Llewellyn Worldwide Ltd. and we will forward your request. Both the author and publisher appreciate hearing from you and learning of your enjoyment of this book and how it has helped you. Llewellyn Worldwide Ltd. cannot guarantee that every letter written to the author can be answered, but all will be forwarded. Please write to:

Sandra Kynes
⁒ Llewellyn Worldwide
2143 Wooddale Drive
Woodbury, MN 55125-2989

Please enclose a self-addressed stamped envelope for reply,
or $1.00 to cover costs. If outside the U.S.A., enclose
an international postal reply coupon.

Many of Llewellyn's authors have websites with additional information and resources. For more information, please visit our website at http://www.llewellyn.com